An Annotated Catalog of
Composers of African Ancestry

AN ANNOTATED CATALOG OF COMPOSERS OF AFRICAN ANCESTRY

Madison H. Carter

VANTAGE PRESS
New York / Washington / Atlanta
Los Angeles / Chicago

FIRST EDITION

Published by Vantage Press, Inc.
516 West 34th Street, New York, New York 10001

Manufactured in the United States of America
ISBN: 0-533-06613-1

Library of Congress Catalog Card No.: 85–90098

To my deceased grandparents,
Mr. and Mrs. Madison J. Bailey;
my mother,
the late Mrs. Ethel M. Furman;
and the late Edmund T. Jenkins

Preface

There is an urgent need for the type of information found in this book. May this tome be a source of inspiration and incentive for many of our musical persons that are conductors, educators, teachers, librarians, writers, et cetera, particularly those of African ancestry. Also, may they choose one of the composers listed within these pages to bring out magazine articles, periodical stories, and even books that have biographical data with complete listings of musical compositions of many of these neglected and forgotten musicians.

Although there is no biographical data in this "labor of love," most of the composers listed can be found in standard references or books now available written by American citizens, mostly of African ancestry.

It is my next aim to follow up this work with another on our jazz arrangers and composers.

An Annotated Catalog of
Composers of African Ancestry

A

ADAMS, ALTON AUGUSTUS (1889–)

Band

The Governor's Own March. Conductor's score.
Carl Fischer, Inc., ©1921. OCLC: 1058280.

Toledo–Lucas County Public Library

For Not Known

Doux Reve D' Amour. A suite of waltzes.
Burt M. Cutler Pub.

Virgin Island March.

ADAMS, LESLIE (1933–)

Ballet

A Kiss in Xanadu.

Choral

Hosanna to the Son Of David. For four-part chorus of mixed voices.
Edited by Frank Pooler.
Walton Music Corp.
Hal Leonard Pub. Corp.

Orchestra

Symphony No. 1.

ADAMS, WELLINGTON ALEXANDER (1879–)

For Not Known

Lyrics of an Humble Birth.
Murray Bros. Printing Co., ©1914.

U.S. Library of Congress; University of Michigan

AKPABOT, SAMUEL EKPE (1931–)

Orchestra

Overture for a Nigerian Ballet. MD.
Oxford University Press.

Scenes from Nigeria. MD.
Oxford University Press.

Three Nigerian Dances. For string orchestra and timpani.
Oxford University Press, ©1977. OCLC: 3853351.

Arizona State University; Georgia State University; Illinois State University; University of Arizona; University of Georgia; University of Illinois; University of New Mexico; University of Tennessee; University of Vermont; Virginia Polytecnic Institute and State University

Vocal

Cynthia's Lament. For soprano and wind orchestra. MD.
Oxford University Press.

ALDRIDGE, AMANDA IRA (1866–1956)

For Not Known

The Arabian Dances.
Chappell & Co., Inc.

Carnival Suite. Five dances.
Chappell & Co., Inc.

Three African Dances.
Chappell & Co., Inc.

AMU, EPHARIM (1899–)

Choral

Twenty-five African Songs in the Twi Language. Music and words by E. Amu. Chiefly for four unaccompanied mixed and men's voices in score. Tshi words.

New York Public Library

ANDERSON, THOMAS JEFFERSON, JR. (1928–)
SEE: American Composers Alliance
170 West 74th Street
New York, NY 10023

C. F. Peters Corp.
373 Park Avenue South
New York, NY 10016

ANDERSON, WALTER FRANKLIN (1915–)

Cantata

Based on President Franklin D. Roosevelt's D-day prayer.

Choral

Prayer Is a Key to Heaven. For four-part chorus of mixed voices with tenor and soprano solos.
Theodore Presser Co.

Choral, Christmas

Aguinaldo (Joseph and Maria). For four-part chorus of mixed voices with piano accompaniment (guitars and maracas ad lib). Venezuelan folk song. s,e. Octavo no. 10541.
G. Schirmer, Inc., ©1957.

Brincan y Bailan (Darting and Dancing). For four-part chorus of mixed voices with piano accompaniment (guitars ad lib). Spanish folk song. s,e. Octavo no. 10540.
G. Schirmer, Inc., ©1957.

El Noi de la Mare? (What Shall We Give?) For four-part chorus of mixed voices a cappella. Ancient carol from Catalonia, Spain. s,e. Octavo no. 10542.
G. Schirmer, Inc., ©1957.

Gatatumba. For four-part chorus of mixed voices with piano accompaniment (clarinet, sleigh bells, tambourine, drum, maracas, and guitar, ad lib). Andalusian carol. s,e. Octavo no. 10511.
G. Schirmer, Inc., ©1957.

Holly Carol, The. For four-part chorus of mixed voices with piano accompaniment. English only. Octavo no. 10824.
G. Schirmer, Inc.

Sing Noel, Merry Noel. For four-part chorus of mixed voices with piano accompaniment. English text only. May be sung a cappella. By John Stainer, arranged by W. F. Anderson. Octavo no. 10682.
G. Schirmer, Inc.

ANDREWS, ISMAY (?)

For Not Known

Tradition. Can be staged with aesthetic dancers.
Handy Bros. Music Co., Inc.

APPLING, WILLIAM (?)

Choral

We Shall Walk through the Valley in Peace. For four-part chorus of men's voices.
World Library Publications, Inc. CE-2328-4.

Yonda' Come Day. For four-part chorus of mixed voices.
World Library Publications, Inc. CE-2329-8.

ARCHER, DUDLEY MALCOLM (1899–1973)

Choral

My Spirit on Thy Care. For four-part chorus of mixed voices. CM7457.
Carl Fischer, Inc.

B

BAKER, DAVID NATHANIEL, JR. (1931–)

SEE: Aamoa Press
2909 Wayzata Blvd.
Minneapolis, MN 55405

Associated Music Pub., Inc.
866 Third Avenue
New York, NY 10022

Dr. David N. Baker, Jr.
3151 Arrow Avenue
Bloomington, IN 47401

Fema Music Pub.
P.O. Box 395
Naperville, IL 60540

Frangipani Press
1928 Arlington Road
Bloomington, IN 47401

Maher Publications, Inc.
222 West Adams
Chicago, IL 60606

Seesaw Music Corp.
1966 Broadway
New York, NY 10023

BALLANTA-TAYLOR, NICHOLAS GEORGE JULIUS (1897–)

Cantata

For chorus and orchestra.

Orchestra

Overture on African Themes.

BANKOLE, AYO (1935–76)

Choral

Three-part Songs. For female choir. First two songs for double chorus (SSA each) a cappella. The third for SSA and piano. Yoruba words. Ile-Ife, Nigeria: University of Ife Press, ©1975.

New York Public Library

Three-part Song. For female choir. Ife music edition. Ile-Ife, Nigeria: University of Ife Press, ©1975. OCLC: 2195567.

Boston University; Illinois State University; Indiana University; Oberlin College

Organ

Toccata and Fugue. Ife music editions no. 8. Ile-Ife, Nigeria: University of Ife Press, ©1978. OCLC: 5970049.

Oberlin College

Piano

Sonata No. 2 in C. Ile-Ife, Nigeria: University of Ife Press, ©1977, OCLC: 5970002.

Oberlin College

Vocal

Three Yoruba Songs. For baritone and piano. Ile-Ife, Nigeria: University of Ife Press, ©1976. OCLC: 5802088

Denver Public Library; Duke University Library; Oberlin College; University of California, San Diego; University of Maryland, Baltimore County

BANKS, ROBERT (1930–)

SEE: Belwin-Mills Pub. Corp.
      25 Deshon Drive
      Melville, NY 11746

BARBOUR, J. BERNI (1881–)

Choral

Doan Let Satan Git You on de Judgment Day.

Done Laid Down All Ma Burden.

I'm Ready to Go.

In-a-de Mornin.

Nicodemus.

Some Day I'm Goin' Home.

Military Musical Revue

Black Propaganda.

Music Extravaganza

Negro Progress.

Redemption.

Opera

Ethopia [*sic*].

Operetta

Arrival of the Negro.

Pageant

Paul Lawrence Dunbar's Dream.

BARÈS, BASILE J. (1845–1902)

Piano

La Belle Créole. Quadrille Des Lanciers Américain.

University of Virginia

La Louisianaise. Valse brillante.
A. E. Blackmar, ©1884. OCLC: 5366463.

Louisiana State University

Les Víolettes, opus 25. In *Piano Music from New Orleans 1851–1898*.
Compiled and with preface by John Baron.
Da Capo Press, ©1980.

University of New Mexico.

BARNES, ERIK S. (1955–)

Piano

Prelude.

SEE: Erik S. Barnes
      N.E. 1025 Monroe
      Pullman, WA 99163

BEARD, IVY LEE (1943–78)

Organ

Lyric Piece.
Manuscript.

BECKON, LETTIE MARIE (1953–)

SEE: Lettie M. Beckon
      16849 Asbury Park
      Detroit, MI 48235

BETHUNE, THOMAS GREEN (1849–1908)

Piano

The Battle of Manassas.
Musica Obscura.

Battle of Manassas. In *Piano Music In Nineteenth Century America*.
Hinshaw Music, Inc., ©1975.

University of New Mexico

Cyclone Gallop.

New York Public Library

Daylight. A musical expression.

Newberry Library, Chicago; University of Illinois; University of Virginia

March Timpani.

U. S. Library of Congress

BILLUPS, KENNETH BROWN (1918–)

Choral

Cert'ly Lord. Negro spiritual. For mixed chorus and piano.
Belwin, Inc., ©1950.

New Born Again. Negro spiritual. For four-part chorus of mixed voices
a cappella.
Belwin, Inc., ©1951.

Southern Illinois University

Swing Low, Sweet Chariot. Negro spiritual. For children's chorus.
G. Schirmer, Inc.

BLEDSOE, JULES C. (1898–1943)

Orchestra

African Suite. For violin and orchestra.

For Not Known

Beside a New-Made Grave.

The Crawfish Song.
Edward B. Marks Music Co., © 1941. OCLC: 4681012.

Oberlin College

Does Ah Love You.

The Farewell.

Grandmother's Melodies.

BOATNER, EDWARD HAMMOND (1898–1981)

Choral

Ride On, King Jesus. Negro spiritual. For mixed chorus.
Franco Colombo, ©1953.

Indiana University

Spirituals Triumphant Old and New.
Sunday School Publishing Board, ©1927.

Howard University; University of New Mexico

9

Musical Comedy

Julius See Her. (Jules Caesar in Rome, Ga.) By E. H. Boatner in collaboration with Gladys Shaw. Erskine & Ivan Firth. Typescript.

New York Public Library

Orchestra

Freedom Suite. For chorus and orchestra.

Howard University

Vocal

I Want Jesus to Walk With me. Negro spiritual. For voice with piano accompaniment.
Galaxy Music Corp., ©1939.

Florida State University

On Ma Journey. Negro spiritual.
G. Ricordi Co., ©1928.

Boston Public Library; Howard University; Indiana University; New York Public Library; U.S. Library of Congress

Trampin'. Negro spiritual. For high voice with piano accompaniment. Also for low voice.
William Maxwell, ©1931.

Boston Public Library

BOLIN, PAUL C. (?)

Choral

The Office for the Holy Communion. For four-part chorus of mixed voices with organ accompaniment.
H. W. Gray Co., ©1920.
Belwin-Mills Pub. Corp.

BONDS, MARGARET ALLISON (1913–72)

Ballet

Migration.
Manuscript, ©1960.

Cantata

The Ballad of the Brown King. For mixed chorus, soli, and piano. Libretto by Langston Hughes.
Sam Fox Pub. Co., ©1961.

Cello

Troubled Water.
Manuscript, © 1964.

Choral

Children's Sleep. For four-part chorus of mixed voices with piano accompaniment. Words by Vernon Glasser.
Carl Fischer, Inc., ©1942.

Yale University, James Weldon Johnson Memorial Collection

Ezek'l Saw the Wheel. For four-part chorus of mixed voices with piano accompaniment.
Mercury Music Corp., ©1966.
Thedore Presser Co.

Go Tell It on the Mountain. For four-part chorus of mixed voices a cappella.
Beekman Music, Inc., ©1962.
Theodore Presser Co.

Hold On. Negro spiritual. For mixed voices with piano accompaniment.
Mercury Music Corp., ©1966.
Theodore Presser Co.

Yale University, James Weldon Johnson Memorial Collection

I Shall Pass through This World. For four-part chorus of mixed voices a cappella.
Bourne Co., ©1967.

Mary Had a Little Baby. (From *The Ballad of the Brown King*.) For women's voices. SSA.
Sam Fox Pub. Co., ©1963.

Mass in D Minor. Latin text. For chorus and orchestra.

The Negro Speaks of Rivers. For four-part chorus of mixed voices with piano accompaniment. Lyrics by Langston Hughes.
Handy Bros. Music Co., Inc., ©1962.

Songs of the Seasons. Song cycle for chorus of male voices. From *Fields of Wonder*. Text by Langston Hughes. Heaven—Snail—Big Sun—Moonlight Night—Carmel—Snake—New Moon—Birth.
Manuscript, ©1960.

You Can Tell the World. For four-part chorus of mixed voices with piano accompaniment.
Mutual Music Society, Inc., ©1957.
Chappell & Co., Inc.

Piano

A Dance in Brown.
Manuscript, ©1931.

Troubled Water.
Sam Fox Pub. Co., ©1967.

Stage Work

Burlesque Is Alive. Music for Inner City Repertory Co.
Production, Los Angeles.

Shakespeare in Harlem. Langston Hughes–Robert Glenn Production.
Manuscript, ©1959.

Vocal

Bright Star. For voice and piano.
Pasea, ©1970.

Didn't It Rain. For medium voice and piano.
Beekman Music, Inc., ©1967.
Theodore Presser Co.

Empty Interlude. For voice and piano.
Robbins Music Corp.

Ezek'l Saw the Wheel. For voice and piano accompaniment or orchestra accompaniment.
Beekman Music, Inc.
Theodore Presser Co., ©1959.

Five Negro Spirituals. For high voice and piano. 1. Dry Bones. 2. I'll Reach to Heaven. 3. Lord, I Just Can't Keep From Cryin'. 4. Sit Down, Servant. 5. You Can Tell the World.
Mutual Music Society, Inc.
Chappell & Co., Inc. © 1946.

New York Public Library

Georgia. For voice and piano. Words and music by M. A. Bonds, Joe Davis, and Andy Razaf.
Georgia Music Corp., ©1939.

Go Tell It on the Mountain. For voice and piano.
Beekman Music, Inc., ©1962.
Theodore Presser Co.

He's Got the Whole World in His Hands. For voice and piano. Also for voice and orchestra.
Beekman Music, Inc., ©1963.
Theodore Presser Co.

I Got a Home in-a That Rock. For voice and piano. Also for voice and orchestra.
Beekman Music, Inc., ©1959.
Theodore Presser Co.

I Shall Pass Through This World. For voice and piano.
Bourne Co., ©1966.

Joshua Fit da Battle of Jericho. For voice and piano. Also for voice and orchestra.
Beekman Music, Inc., ©1967.
Theodore Presser Co.

Mary Had a Little Baby. From *The Ballad of the Brown King*. For voice and piano. ©1962.

The Negro Speaks of Rivers. For voice and piano.
Handy Bros. Music Co., Inc., ©1942.

Yale University, James Weldon Johnson Memorial Collection

Peach Tree Street. Blues song. For voice and piano. Words and music by M. A. Bonds, Joe Davis, and Andy Razaf.
Georgia Music Corp., ©1939.

Rainbow Gold. For voice and piano. Words by Roger Chaney.
Chappell & Co., Inc., ©1956.

Sing A-Ho That I Had the Wings of a Dove. For voice and piano.
Chappell & Co., Inc., ©1960.

Sinner, Please Don't Let This Harvest Pass. For voice and piano.
Manuscript, ©1970.

Spring Will Be So Sad. For voice and piano. Words by Harold Dickinson.
Mutual Music Society, Inc.
Chappell & Co., Inc., ©1941.

New York Public Library

Three Dream Portraits. For high voice and piano. 1. Dream Variation.
2. I, Too. 3. Minstrel Man. Words by Langston Hughes.
G. Ricordi & Co., ©1959.
Belwin-Mills Pub. Co.

Yale University, James Weldon Johnson Memorial Collection.

Three Sheep In A Pasture. For voice and piano.
Clarence Williams Music Co., ©1940.

To a Brown Girl Dead. For high voice. Words by Countee Cullen.
R. D. Row Music Co., ©1956.   •
Carl Fischer, Inc.

When The Dove Enters In. A gospel song. For voice and piano. Words
by Langston Hughes.
Sam Fox Pub. Co.

Yale University, James Weldon Johnson Memorial Collection

You Can Tell the World. Negro spiritual. For voice and orchestra.
Mutual Music Society, ©1946.

BONNEMARE, EDWARD VALENTINE (1921–)
SEE: Amity Music Corp.
        1475 Gaylor Terrace
        Teaneck, NJ 07666

        Fortress Press
        2900 Queen Lane
        Philadelphia, PA 19129

BROWN, J. HAROLD (1902–)

Cantata

African Chief. For female voices with concert band accompaniment.

Oratorio

Job.

String Quartet

A minor.

For Not Known

Allegro.

Autumn Moods.

Prestidigitation.

Rhapsody.

SEE: Handy Bros. Music Co., Inc.
        200 West 72nd Street
        New York, NY 10023

BROWN, LAWRENCE (1893–1972)

Cello

Five Negro Folk Songs. Piano accompaniment.
London: Schott & Co., Ltd., ©1923.

Indiana University

————. Microfilm (master negative).

New York Public Library

Vocal

Five Negro Spirituals. For voice with piano accompaniment.
London: Schott & Co., Ltd., ©1924.

I'm Goin' to Tell God All My Troubles. Negro spiritual. No. 4 of Six
Negro Folk Songs. For voice with piano accompaniment.
Associated Music Pub., Inc., ©1943.

University of Southern California

Negro Folk Songs. For voice with piano accompaniment. 1. Didn't My Lord Deliver Daniel? 2. Who's Been Here? 3. Hear de Lam's A-crying'. 4. Goin' to Ride Up in de Chariot. 5. Dare's a Man Goin' Roun' Takin' Names.
London: Schott & Co., Ltd., ©1930.

Boston Public Library; Brown University; University of Southern California; Yale University, James Weldon Johnson Memorial Collection

Six Negro Folk Songs. For medium voice with piano accompaniment. 1. Great Gittin' Up Mornin'. 2. Hammer Song. 3. I Got a Robe. 4. I'm Goin' to Tell God All My Troubles. 5. No More. 6. Poor Wayfarin' Stranger.
Associated Music Pub., Inc., ©1943.

U.S. Library of Congress; Yale University, James Weldon Johnson Memorial Collection

Spirituals. Five Negro Songs. For voice with piano accompaniment. 1. Nobody Knows de Trouble I've Seen. 2. Sometimes I Feel like a Motherless Child. 3. I Know de Lord's Laid His Hands on Me. 4. Swing Low, Sweet Chariot. 5. Ev'ry Time I Feel de Spirit.
London: Schott & Co., Ltd., ©1923.

Brown University; New York Public Library; Yale University, James Weldon Johnson Memorial Collection

Steal Away. Negro folk song. For voice with piano accompaniment.
London: W. Rogers, Ltd., ©1922.

Yale University, James Weldon Johnson Memorial Collection

BURLEIGH, HARRY THACKER (1866–1949)

Choral

Old Songs Hymnal. For chorus of mixed voices. Words and melodies from the state of Georgia. Collected by Dorothy G. Bolton. Music arranged by H. T. Burleigh.
The Century Co., ©1929. OCLC: 4969002.

Dallas Public Library; Iliff School of Theology, Denver

Violin

Deep River. Negro spiritual. Piano accompaniment.
G. Ricordi, ©1917. Publ. pl. no. 116379.3.

Indiana University

Southland Sketches. (Four.) Piano accompaniment.
G. Ricordi, ©1916. Publ. pl. nos. 116310–116313.

New York Public Library

Vocal

Plantation Songs. For voice with piano accompaniment.
Franco Colombo, ©1902. Publ. pl. no. 15894.

Saracen Songs. For voice with piano accompaniment.
G. Ricordi & Co., ©1914. Publ. pl. no. 114181.

The Young Warrior (Il giovane querriero). For voice with piano accompaniment. Also voice alone. Poem by James Weldon Johnson. Italian text by Edoardo Petro.
G. Ricordi & Co., ©1915.

Yale University, James Weldon Johnson Memorial Collection

BUTLER, FRANK S. (1883–1967)

Book

The Master School of Professional Piano Playing. Rag, jazz, blues, popular, semiclassical, and classical. . . .
Butler Music Co., ©1925.

Cleveland Public Library

For Not Known

Blossoms.
Emil Ascher, ©1927.

C

CALHOUN, W. ARTHUR (?)

Choral

Down in the Valley A-waiting for My Jesus. For mixed voices.
Handy Bros. Music Co., Inc.

CARTER, JOHN (1937–)
SEE: American Music Center, Inc.
250 West 54th Street
Room 300
New York, NY 10019

Peer-Southern Organization
1740 Broadway
New York, NY 10019

CASSEUS, FRANTZ GABRIEL (1921–)

Guitar

Dance of the Hounsies.
Franco Colombo.
Belwin-Mills Pub. Corp.

CERON, JOSÉ DOLORES (1897–)

Vocal

Himno del ejectito dominocano. For voice with piano accompaniment.
Ciudad Trujillo: Letra de Emilia A. Morel., © 1938.

CHARLTON, MELVILLE (1880–1973)

Book

The Evolution of Negro Music. New York State Commission, National Negro Exposition. Richmond, Virginia, 1915. Schomburg microfilm no. 154 negative. OCLC: 2394161.

Kent State University
Musical Therapeuties, n.p., 1940, 7 p.

Piano

Poeme Erotique.
G. Schirmer, Inc., ©1934.

Yale University, James Weldon Johnson Memorial Collection

Organ

Double Fugue In E Minor.
Manuscript.

CHEATHAM, WALLACE (1945–)

Choral

My Soul Is a Witness. Negro spiritual. For eight-part chorus of mixed voices a cappella.
Shawnee Press, Inc.

CHILDS, JOHN, JR. (?)

Organ

Prelude.
Manuscript, ©1974.

SEE: John Childs Jr.
128 Lafayette Avenue
Brooklyn, NY 11238

CHRISTY, OTTO MAE JONES (1920–)

Choral

A Collection of Negro Spirituals. For chorus of mixed voices.

CLARK, EDGAR ROGIE (1913–78)

19

Ballet

The Lonely Island.

Band

John Henry Fantasy.

Cello

Figurine. Piano accompaniment.

Choral

Mango Walk. For four-part chorus of mixed voices with piano accompaniment. Octavo no. 5101.
Boosey & Hawkes, Inc.

Sit Down, Servant. Negro spiritual. For four-part chorus of mixed a cappella. Octavo no. 5067.
Boosey & Hawkes, Inc.

Clarinet

Fantasia. Piano accompaniment.

Collection

Copper Sun. Negro folk music.
Theodore Presser Co.

Opera

The Stranger. One act (four soloists, no chorus).
Ti Yette. One act (chamber orchestra).

Orchestra

Elegia. For string orchestra.

Fete Creole.

Larghetto. For string orchestra.

Organ

Prelude Bachinegras. Arranged by Eugene Wilson Hancock.
Manuscript.

String Quartet

Divertimento.

Vocal

Negro Art Songs. Album of contemporary composers. For voice with piano accompaniment.
Edward B. Marks Music Corp., ©1946.

Atlanta University; Indiana University; Tuskegee Institute; Yale University, James Weldon Johnson Memorial Collection

For Not Known

The Myrtle Tree.

Prelude for Wednesday.

CLARKE, BONNA MAE PERINE (?)

Choral

A Collection of Negro Spirituals. For chorus of mixed voices with piano accompaniment.
Handy Bros. Music Co., Inc., ©1939.

Brown University; Cleveland Public Library; Free Library of Philadelphia; Michigan State Library; Union Catalogue of Pennsylvania; U. S. Library of Congress; University of Iowa

CLARY, SALONE THEODORE (1939–)

SEE: Warner Bros. Publications, Inc.
        75 Rockefeller Plaza
        New York, NY 10019

CLAY, OMAR (?)

Flute

Three Short Pieces.

COCHRAN, ARTHUR MYRON (1878–)

Choral

Communion Service in F. Major. For chorus of mixed voices with organ accompaniment.

Office of the Holy Communion of the Protestant Espiscopal Church in the U.S.A. Music founded on Negro spirituals, ©1925.

Yale University, James Weldon Johnson Memorial Collection

COLEMAN, CHARLES D. (1926–)

Choral

Alleluia. For four-part chorus of mixed voices a cappella.
Northwestern School of Music Press, © 1976.

Blest Be the Tie. For four-part chorus of mixed voices a cappella.
Northwestern School of Music Press, ©1977.

The Lord's Prayer. For four-part chorus of mixed voices a cappella.
Northwestern School of Music Press, ©1964.

O Perfect Love. For four-part chorus of mixed voices with piano accompaniment.
Northwestern School of Music Press, ©1977.

Seeking for That City. For four-part chorus of mixed voices a cappella.
Northwestern School of Music Press, ©1977.

Organ

Impromptu. (For pedals alone.)
Northwestern School of Music Press, ©1961.

Sonata No. 1.
Northwestern School of Music Press, ©1979.

COLERIDGE-TAYLOR, AVRIL GWENDOLEN (1903–)

Choral

Wyndore (Windover). Arranged for four-part chorus of mixed voices and orchestra.
J. & W. Chester, Ltd., ©1936.

U.S. Library of Congress

COLERIDGE-TAYLOR, SAMUEL (1875–1912)

Chamber Orchestra

Charasteristic Waltzes. Valse de la reine. (No. 3 of 4.) Kalmus chamber music series V9440. For two violins, viola, cello, and piano. Edwin F. Kalmus.

North Texas State University

Four Novelletten. Opus 52. For string orchestra. London: Novello & Co., Ltd.

Edwin A. Fleisher Music Collection

Orchestra

The Bamboula. Rhapsodic dance no. 1. Boosey & Hawkes, Inc., ©1911.

New York Public Library

Christmas Overture. Arranged by Sidney Baynes. Boosey & Hawkes, Inc.

Danse Negre. Opus 35, no. 4. Augener, Ltd.

Edwin A. Fleisher Music Collection

Faust. Incidental music. Opus 70. Boosey & Hawkes, Inc., ©1908.

Yale University, James Weldon Johnson Memorial Collection

Hiawatha's Wedding Feast. Arranged by W. G. Ross. London: Novello & Co., Ltd.

Edwin A. Fleisher Music Collection

Nero. Incidental music. London: Novello & Co., Ltd.

Romance In G Major. For violin and orchestra. London: Novello & Co., Ltd.

Edwin A. Fleisher Music Collection

Saint Agnes' Eve Suite. Boosey & Hawkes, Inc.

Scenes from an Imaginary Ballet. Suite. Arranged by Elliot F. Schenk Boosey & Hawkes, Inc.

Symphonic Variation on an African Air. Opus 63.
London: Novello & Co., Ltd.

Edwin A. Fleisher Music Collection

Organ

Organ Album. 1. Processional from Herod. 2. Cameo. 3. Second Impromtu. 4. Sorrow Song, no. 2. 5. Idyll. 6. Ethiopia Saluting the Co-Coulours. Arranged by Dr. A. Eaglefield Hull. London: Augener, Ltd., ©1916.

University of Illinois

Three Impromtus. Opus 78.
London: A. Weeks, ©1911.

Indiana University

The Villiage Organist. 1. Arietta in F. 2. Elegy in G Minor. 3. Melody in D.
London: Novello & Co., Ltd.

Violin Concerto In G Minor. Arranged by J. Stuart Archer.

Piano

Three Humoresques. Opus 31. Edition no. 6102.
London: Augener, Ltd. OCLC: 4116861.

Yale University, James Weldon Johnson Memorial Collection; Washington University, St. Louis, Missouri

Piano Duet

Three-fours. Valse suite. Opus 71. Arranged by Alex Roloff. Book nos. 1–3. Book nos. 4–5.
London: Augener, Ltd., ©1918.

University of New Mexico

Violin

Four African Dances. Opus 58. Piano accompaniment. Edition no. 11342.
London: Augener, Ltd., ©1904. OCLC: 5216438.

Violin Album. Six easy pieces arranged by B. C. Hull. 1. A June Rose Bloomed. 2. Neurmahal's Song. 3. Scène de Ballet. 4. Zarifa. 5. Regret. 6. Ethiopia March.
London: Augener, Ltd.

Vocal

Seven African Romances. For voice with piano accompaniment. Edition no. 8817.
London: Augener, Ltd., ©1897.

Free Library of Philadelphia

COOK, WILL MARION (1869–1944)

Opera

In Dahomey.
London: Prowse, Keith Music Pub. Co., Ltd. Publ. pl. no. 1570.

New York Public Library, Schomburg Collection

COOKE, CHARLES L. (1891–1958)

Choral

Robbins Choral Collection. Negro spirituals. For chorus of mixed voices with piano accompaniment.
1. Deep River.
2. Give Me That Old Time Religion.
3. Go Down Moses.
4. Gospel Train.
5. Heav'n, Heav'n.
6. Joshua Fit de Battle of Jericho.
7. Nobody the Trouble I've Had.
8. Sometimes I Feel like a Motherless Child.
9. Steal Away.
10. Swing Low, Sweet Chariot.
11. We Are Climbing Jacob's Ladder.
Robbins Music Corp., ©1942.
Big 3 Music Corp.

Orchestra

Pro Arte. An overture.

COOPER, WILLIAM BENJAMIN (1920–)

Cantata

The Beatitudes. For four-part chorus of mixed voices with soprano, alto, and tenor solo. Organ accompaniment. Manuscript, ©1966.

New York Public Library

Choral

The Port Royal Te Deum. For solo quartet, soli, chorus, dance with percussion and organ.
Dangerfield Music Co., ©1970.

New York Public Library

The Psalms and Canticles. According to the use of the Protestant Episcopal Church, pointed and set to African American chants, together with the choral service. For four-part chorus of mixed voices.
Organ accompaniment and a cappella.
Dangerfield Music Co., ©1969 and 197—

New York Public Library

Organ

Arrangement of Traditional Negro Spirituals.
Manuscript with pencil corrections.

Indiana University

Bread of Heaven.
Dangerfield Music Co.

Meditation on Steal Away. Negro spiritual.
Manuscript.

Indiana University

Pastorale.
Manuscript, ©1973.

Procession Liturgique.
Manuscript.

Symphony.
Manuscript.

Toccatina.
Dangerfield Music Co.

Organ and Cello

Fantasy.
Manuscript.

CORDERO, ROQUE (1917–)

Orchestra

Eight Minatures. For chamber orchestra.
Reproduced from manuscript, ©1948.

New York Public Library

Movimiento Sinfonico. For string orchestra.
Reproduced from manuscript, ©1946.

New York Public Library

Rapsodie Campesina.
Manuscript, ©1949.

U.S. Library of Congress

Piano

Sonatina Ritmica.
Pan American Union.
Peer-Southern Organization, ©1954.

Peabody Institute; New York Public Library; U.S. Library of Congress; University of California, Los Angeles; University of Iowa; University of Michigan; University of North Carolina

String Quartet

Danza En Forma De Fuga.
Independent Music Pub., ©1943.

New York Public Library

CROWDER, HENRY (?)

Vocal

Henry Music. Collection of songs. For voice.
Paris: Hours Press, ©1930. OCLC: 1933041.

Boston Public Library; Brown University; New York Public Library; Ohio State University; Southern Illinois University; University of Michigan; Yale Univer-

sity, *James Weldon Johnson Memorial Collection; Miami University, Oxford University; Southern Illinois University; Univ of Nebraska–Lincoln; University of Texas at Austin; Washington University, Saint Louis, Missouri*

CUNNINGHAM, ARTHUR H. (1928–)

Choral

SEE: Theodore Presser Co.
       Bryn Mawr, PA 19010

Opera

His Natural Grace.

An opera for children.

Orchestra

SEE: Theodore Presser Co. Rental library of orchestral and instrumental music.

Organ

Prelude.
Manuscript, ©1965.

D

DA COSTA, NOEL GEORGE (1929–)

Cello

Five Verses/with Vamps. Piano accompaniment.
King's Crown Music Press, ©1976.
Galaxy Music Corp.

University of New Mexico

Organ

Chilí-lo. An East African lament.
Manuscript, ©1971.

Maryton. Hymn tune variations.
Manuscript, ©1955.

Spiritual Set. Four movements: Invocation. Affirmation. Spiritual—'Round
about the Mountain. Praise.
H. W. Gray Co., Inc., ©1977.
Belwin-Mills Pub. Corp.

University of New Mexico

Triptych. Three movements: Prelude. Processional. Postlude.
Manuscript, ©1973.

Organ and Percussion

Ukom Memory Songs.
Manuscript, ©1981.

Organ and Strings

Generata.
Manuscript, ©1958.

SEE: Atsco Music Pub.
Noel G. Da Costa
Rutgers University
Newark, NJ 07102

DAVIS, ELMER L. (1926–)

Choral

You Gotta Cross the River When You Die. For four-part chorus of mixed voices a cappella.
G. Schirmer, Inc., ©1958.

DAWSON, WILLIAM LEVI (1899–)

Choral

Ezekiel Saw de Wheel. For four-part chorus of mixed voices a cappella.
Neil A. Kjos Music Co., ©1942.

Peabody Institute

I Couldn't Hear Nobody Pray. For four-part chorus of mixed voices and soprano solo a cappella.
H. T. FitzSimons Co., Inc., ©1926.

Southern Illinois University

King Jesus Is A-Listening. For four-part chorus of mixed voices a cappella.
H. T. FitzSimons Co., Inc., ©1925.

Southern Illinois University

Lit'l' Boy-chile. For four-part chorus of mixed voices with soprano, baritone, and base solos a cappella.
Neil A. Kjos Music Co., ©1942.

Peabody Institute

Mary Had a Baby. For four-part chorus of men's voices with tenor solo a cappella.
Neil A. Kjos Music Co., ©1947.

Mary Had a Baby. For four-part chorus of mixed voices with soprano solo a cappella.
Neil A. Kjos Music Co., ©1947.

Southern Illinois University

Soon Ah Will Be Done. For four-part chorus of men's voices a cappella.
Neil A. Kjos Music Co., ©1934.

University of Illinois

Soon Ah Will Be Done. For four-part chorus of mixed voices a cappella.
Neil A. Kjos Music Co., ©1947.

Yale University, James Weldom Johnson Memorial Collection

Steal Away. For four-part chorus of men's voices with tenor solo a cappella.
Neil A. Kjos Music Co., ©1942.

University of Illinois

Steal Away. For four-part chorus of mixed voices a cappella.
Neil A. Kjos Music Co., ©1942.

Yale University, James Weldom Johnson Memorial Collection

Swing Low, Sweet Chariot. For four-part chorus of men's voices a cappella.
Neil A. Kjos Music Co., ©1946.

Swing Low, Sweet Chariot. For four-part chorus of mixed voices with soprano solo a cappella.
Neil A. Kjos Music Co., ©1949.

Southern Illinois University

Swing Low, Sweet Chariot. For three-part chorus of women's voices with soprano solo a cappella.
Neil A. Kjos Music Co., ©1949.

There Is a Balm in Gilead. For four-part chorus of men's voices with tenor solo a cappella.
Neil A. Kjos Music Co., ©1939.

There Is a Balm in Gilead. For four-part chorus of women's voices with soprano solo a cappella.
Neil A. Kjos Music Co., ©1939.

Yale University, James Weldom Johnson Memorial Collection

There Is a Balm in Gilead. For three-part chorus of women's voices with soprano solo a cappella.
Neil A. Kjos Music Co., ©1939.

Orchestra

A Negro Work Song.
Photocopy.

New York Public Library

Symphony No. 1 in E-flat Major.
Negative photostat of manuscript.

Yale University, James Weldon Johnson Memorial Collection

Piano

Interlude.
Positive photostat of manuscript.

New York Public Library; Yale University, James Weldon Johnson Memorial Collection

DE PAUR, LEONARD (1914–)

Choral

SEE: Lawson-Gould Music Pub., Inc.
866 Third Avenue
New York, NY 10022

Oratorio

Haiti. Complete working score by William Du Bois.
Random House, ©1938. OCLC: 1284184. 171063.

Brown University; Detroit Public Library; Grosvenor Reference Division, Buffalo and Erie County Public Library; New York Public Library; New Mexico State University

DÉDÉ, EDMUND (1827–1903)

Opera

Le Sultan d' Isphan. A four-act opera.

For Not Known

Le Serment de l'Arabe.

Patriotisme.

Quasimodo Symphony.

Si j'étais lui.

Valliant Belle Rose Quadrille (later called Le Palmier Overture).

DENNIS, NORTON EDWARD (?)

Operetta

Mandalay.

DETT, ROBERT NATHANIEL (1882–1943)

Collection

The Dett Collection of Negro Spirituals. Some never before in print. Anthems, motets, and mixed-voice settings. For four-part chorus of mixed voices a cappella. Some with piano accompaniment. The H. & M. Auditorium Series. First Group—Second Group—Third Group—Fourth Group.
Schmitt, Hall & McCreary Co., ©1936.
Belwin-Mills Pub. Corp.

Oratorio

The Ordering Of Moses. For four-part chorus of mixed voices with soprano, alto, tenor, and baritone solos with orchestra accompaniment.
J. Fischer & Bro., ©1939.
Belwin-Mills Pub. Corp.

Yale University, James Weldon Johnson Memorial Collection

Orchestra

An American Sampler.
Manuscript.

Enchantment Suite.
Manuscript.

Edwin A. Fleisher Music Collection

Listen to the Lambs. Fantasia for violin and orchestra.
Manuscript.

Symphony In E Minor.
Manuscript.

33

Tropic Winter Suite.
Manuscript.

Organ

The Deserted Cabin. (From Magnolia Suite.)
Arranged by Gordon Balch Nevin.
Clayton F. Summy Co., ©1918.
Summy-Brichard Co.

Library Association of Portland, Oregon

Mammy. (From Magnolia Suite.)
Arranged by Gordon Balch Nevin.
Clayton F. Summy Co., ©1918.
Summy-Birchard Co.

Boston Public Library

Violin

Ramah. Piano accompaniment.
Boston Music Co.

For Not Known

Follow Me. Negro spiritual from collection of Mrs. Catherine Fields-Gay.
Arranged by R. N. Dett.
John Church Co., ©1919.
Theodore Presser Co. OCLC: 7642668.

Duke University Library

Negro Spirituals. With music and melodies harmonized.
London: Blanford Press, ©1959.

Yale University, James Weldon Johnson Memorial Collection

DICKERSON, ROGER DONALD (1934–)

Orchestra

Concert Overture.
Manuscript.

SEE: Peer-Southern Organization
        1740 Broadway
        New York, NY 10019

Organ

Chorale Prelude. Das neugeborne kindelein.

Indiana University

DILL, WILLIAM LESLIE (1913–)

Band

Modeerf. Chant spiritualistic. Symphonic.
Elkan-Vogel, Inc., ©1966. OCLC: 1107705.

Kent State University

DINROE, DOROTHY (?)

For Not Known

Children's Game.

DITON, CARL ROSSINI (1886–1962)

Choral

Four Jubilee Songs. For five-part chorus of mixed voices a cappella. 1. Deep River. 2. Ev'ry Time I Feel The Spirit. 3. Little David, Play on Your Harp. 4. Pilgrim's Song.
G. Schirmer, Inc., ©1915.
Publ. pl. nos. 25011, 25491–25493.

New York Public Library

Thirty-six South Carolina Spirituals Collected and Harmonized. For four voices with music.
G. Schirmer Inc., ©1930.
Publ. pl. no. 34759.

Boston Public Library; Brown University; Cleveland Public Library; Cornell University; Fisk University; Free Library of Philadelphia; Indiana University; Newberry Library, Chicago; New York Public Library; Tennessee State Library and Archives; University of Chicago; University of Iowa

Orchestra

Symphony in C Minor.

Organ

Fantasy on Swing Low, Sweet Chariot. Negro spiritual. An arrangement.
G. Schirmer, Inc.

Keep Me from Sinking Down. Negro melody. An arrangement.
G. Schirmer, Inc., ©1921.

Boston Public Library; Library Association of Portland, Oregon

Piano

Rhapsody in E Major. Opus 1, no. 3.
Reproduced from manuscript., ©1912.

New York Public Library

Vocal

A Collection of Negro Part Songs. Piano accompaniment for rehearsal
only. 1. An' He Never Spoke a Mumbelin' Word. 2. At The Beautiful
Gate. 3. Deep River. 4. Little David, Play on Your Harp. 5. Poor Mourn-
er's Got a-Home at Last. 6. Roll, Jordan, Roll.
G. Schirmer, Inc., ©1915–21.

Boston Public Library; New York Public Library

For Not Known

Ballade in E Major.

The Hymn of Nebraska.

DORSEY, JAMES ELMO (1905–)

Orchestra

An American Vignette. A full choral symphony in four movements.
Theodore Presser Co., ©1945.

Indiana University

String Quartet

Theme and Variation.

Vocal

Aria. For baritone with orchestra accompaniment.

For Not Known

Sandols.

Sonata.

DORSEY, THOMAS ANDREW (1899–)

Gospel

SEE: OCLC

DUNBAR, RUDOLPH (1907–)

Ballet

Dance of the Twenty-first Century.

Book

Treatise on the Clarinet. Boehm system.
London: J. E. Dallas. OCLC: 2322942.

Harvard University; New York Public Library, Schomburg Collection; Boston Public Library; Southern Illinois University; U.S. Library of Congress; University of Massachusetts; University of North Carolina at Greensboro; Vancouver Public Library; Brandeis University; California State University, Northridge; Carnegie Library of Pittsburgh; Central Michigan University; Central State University; Evangel College; Free Library of Philadelphia; George Washington University; Knox College; Mankato State University; Millersville State College; SUNY College at Purchase; University of Georgia; University of Maryland; University of Michigan; University of North Carolina, Greensboro; Wichita State University; Youngstown State University

DUNCAN, JOHN (1913–75)

Cantata

Burial of Moses. For four-part chorus of mixed voices with alto soloist and wind instruments.
Manuscript, ©1972.

Choral

An Easter Canticle. For four-part chorus of mixed voices and wind instruments.
Manuscript.

You're Tired, Chile. For four-part chorus of mixed voices with tenor solo. Piano accompaniment.
Standard Music Publications, ©1972.

Opera

Gideon and Eliza.

The Hellish Bandit.

Orchestra

Concerto. Trombone and orchestra.

Pagan Impulse. Symphonic poem in D.

String Quartet

Atavistic.

Vocal

Atavisms. For voice, brass, and percussion.

Indiana University

SEE: Mrs. Dorothy Duncan Shepherd
      3418 East 104th Street
      Kansas City, MO 64137

E

EL DABH, HALIM (1921–)

Choral

Lamentations de Pharaon. For chorus of women's voices with soprano and baritone solos. Orchestra accompaniment. Text by Halim El-Dabh. C. F. Peters Corp. OCLC: 1382763.

Kent State University

Pyramide. (Pierre jusqu'au ciel.) For four-part chorus of men's voices with orchestra accompaniment. Text by Halim El-Dabh. P6354. C. F. Peters Corp. OCLC: 1910487

Kent State University

Orchestra

Bacchanalia. Minature score. P6179. C. F. Peters Corp. OCLC: 619806.

California State University, Hayward; Free Library of Philadelphia; Illinois Wesleyan University; Kent State University; Northern Illinois University; SUNY College at Potsdam; SUNY College at Purchase; University of Cincinnati; University of Southern California

Percussion

Fantasis-Tahmeel. For timpani and strings. C. F. Peters Corp. OCLC: 1378211.

Kent State University

Hindi-Yaat No. 1. 3 to 5, or 6, 9, 10, or 12 players. P6197. C. F. Peter Corp. OCLC: 1292454

Carnegie Library of Pittsburgh; Dartmouth College; East Carolina University; Governors State University; Kent State University; Southern Illinois University; SUNY College at Fredonia; University of California, Irvine; University of Kentucky; University of Maryland; University of Pittsburgh; Virginia Commonwealth University

Mosaic No. 1. Piano and percussion. Double traps. 3 or 5 players. P6994.
C. F. Peters Corp. OCLC: 1249741.

Ball State University; Bowdoin College; Cameron University; Dartmouth College; Illinois Wesleyan University; Kent State University; University of Pittsburgh

Sonic No. 7, No. 10. For Derabucca drum (timpani). P6186.
C. F. Peters Corp. OCLC: 1047822.

Cleveland State University; Illinois Wesleyan University; Kent State University; SUNY College at Fredonia; University of California, Irvine; University of Houston; University of Nebraska–Lincoln; University of Pittsburgh

Tabla Dance. For piano and percussion ensemble. P6194.
C. F. Peters Corp. OCLC: 2484096.

Cameron University; Dartmouth College; Kent State University; Louisiana State University; Middlebury College; SUNY College at Fredonia; University of California, Irvine; University of Houston; University of Pittsburgh

Tabla Tahmeel No. 1. P6196.
C. F. Peters Corp. OCLC: 1039053.

California Institute of the Arts; Dartmouth College; Illinois State University; Kent State University; SUNY College at Fredonia; University of Arizona; University of California, Irvine; University of California, La Jolla; University of California, Los Angeles; University of New Mexico; University of Pittsburgh

Piano

Mekta in the Art Of Kita. Two volumes.

I. Books 1 and 2. P6184.

II. Book 3. P6185.

   C. F. Peters Corp. OCLC: 681470.

Bradley University; Buffalo and Erie County Public Library; California State

University, Dominquez Hills; Dartmouth College; Indiana University; Kent State University; Lee College; Lewis and Clark College; Smith College; SUNY College at Fredonia; University of Maryland; University of Pittsburgh; University of Richmond

Vocal

Yulei. The ghose. For female voice, oboe, clarinet in A, trumpet, horn, and strings. High voice.
C. F. Peters Corp. OCLC: 1376891.

Kent State University

ELIE, JUSTIN (1883–1931)

Ballet

Voudou.

Band

The Queen of the Night. From the Babylon suite.
Carl Fischer, Inc.

New York Public Library

Orchestra

Babylon (Nuit Babylonienne). A suite of four Original sketches. 1. Bayaderes. 2. Odalisks. 3. Queen of the Night. 4. Orgy. Arranged by Charles J. Roberts. Piano conductor score.
Carl Fischer, Inc., ©1925. Publ. pl. no. 23583–86.

New York Public Library

Indian Dance and Ritual. Piano-conductor score.
Belwin, Inc., ©1929. Publ. pl. no. B.C.E. no. 134.
Belwin-Mills Pub. Corp.

New York Public Library

Kiskaya (Suite Aborigene). In four parts. Piano-conductor score.
Carl Fischer, Inc., ©1928. Publ. pl. nos. 24561,24562,24569,24639.

New York Public Library

Les Chants de la Montagne (Ancient Mountain Legend). Nocturne. Arranged from original score by Charles J. Roberts. Piano conductor score.

Carl Fischer, Inc., ©1927. Publ. pl. no. 24131.

Melida. A creole tropical dance. Arranged by Charles J. Roberts.
Carl Fischer, Inc., ©1927. Publ. pl. no. 24318.

Night in the Andes (La nuit dans les Andes). Piano-conductor score.
Carl Fischer, Inc., ©1930. Publ. pl. no. 25531.

The Queen of the Night. From the Babylon suite. Arranged by Charles J. Roberts.
Carl Fischer, Inc., ©1928, Publ. pl. no. 24517.

Rumba. From Spanish Colonial Sketches. Piano conductor score.
Belwin, Inc., ©1929. Publ. pl. no. B.C.E. no. 133.
Belwin-Mills Pub. Corp.

Piano

Indian Dance and Ritual.
Belwin, Inc., ©1929. Publ. pl. no. 94.
Belwin-Mills Pub. Corp.

Meringues. Populaires Haitiennes Arrangees et Harmonisees.

Nocturne. Les Chants de la Montagne, no. 3.
Carl Fischer, Inc., ©1923. Publ. pl. no. 22890.

Rumba. From Spanish Colonial Sketches.
Belwin, Inc., ©1929. Publ. pl. no. 93.
Belwin-Mills Pub. Corp.

Rustic Scherzo. Also organ.
T. B. Harms Co.

Violin

Haitian Legend. Piano accompaniment.
G. Schirmer, Inc.

Boston Public Library

For Not Known

The Echo.

Boston Public Library

ELKINS, WILLIAM CUTHBERT (1872–)

Male Quartet

Dere's a Man Goin' 'Round Takin' Names.
Handy Bros. Music Co., Inc.

Remember and Be Careful Every Day.
Handy Bros. Music Co., Inc.

Time Ain't Long.
Handy Bros. Music Co., Inc.

EUBA, AKIN (1935–)

Percussion

Igi Nia So. For Yoruba drums and piano. Oriki score.
Ibadan: Mbari Publications.

New York Public Library

Piano

Scenes from Traditional Life.
Ile-Ife, Nigeria: University of Ife Press, ©1975. OCLC: 2195651.

Boston University; Illinois State University; Indiana University; New York Public Library; Oberlin College; San Jose State University; University of Illinois

Vocal

Six Yoruba Folk Songs. Arranged for voice and piano.
Ile-Ife, Nigeria: University of Ife Press.

New York Public Library

Three Songs. For voice, piano, and Iyalu drum. 1. Agbe. 2. Eiye Meta. 3. Nighati Mo Gho Rohin. Yoruba words. Oriki scores.
Ibadan; Mbari Publications.

New York Public Library

EUBANKS, RACHEL A. (?)

Cantata

Ode to Faith. For chorus, solos, with orchestra accompaniment. Text from Scripture. English words.
Reproduced from manuscript, ©1947 (?).

New York Public Library

EVANTI, LILLIAN (1890–1967)

Choral

My Little Prayer. For mixed voices. Poem by Mrs. Bruce Evans. Arranged by Charles L. Cooke.
Handy Bros. Music Co., Inc.

Slow Me Down Lawd. For mixed voices. Poem by Minna Mathison. Arranged by Charles L. Cooke.
Handy Bros. Music Co., Inc..

Vocal

Himno Pan-Americano. For voice with piano accompaniment. Text by Alice Anderson.
©1941.

New York Public Library

Dedication. For voice with piano accompaniment. Poem by Georgia Douglas Johnson.
Handy Bros. Music Co., Inc.

The Mighty Rapture. For voice with piano accompaniment. Poem by Edwin Mark from *Victory in Defeat.*
Handy Bros. Music Co., Inc.

Speak To Him Thou. For voice with piano accompaniment. Poem by Alfred Tennyson from The Higher Pantheism. Dedicated to Marion Anderson.
Handy Bros. Music Co., Inc.

Tomorrow's World. For voice with piano accompaniment. Words by Georgia Douglas Johnson. Dedicated to World's Peace. Columbian Music Co., ©1948.

United Nations. For voice with piano accompaniment. Words and music by Lillian Evanti.
Lillian Evanti, Publisher.
SEE: Columbian Music Co.—Lillian Evanti Pub.
The Evans-Tibbs Collection
Thurlow Evans Tibbs, Jr., Director
1910 Vermont Avenue, N.W.
Washington, D. C. 20001

Edward B. Marks Music Corp.
1790 Broadway
New York, New York 10019

Handy Brothers Music Co., Inc.
Broadway at 200 West 72nd St.
New York, NY 10023

F

FAX, MARK (1911–74)

Organ

Three Pieces.
Manuscript.

Piano

Toccatina. In: Panorama, *Collection of seventeen American pieces*, intermediate. Compiled and edited by Alice McElroy Procter.
The American Music Co., ©1953.

University of New Mexico

SEE: Augsburg Publishing House
       426 South Fifth Street
       Minneapolis, MN 55415

       G. Schirmer, Inc.
       866 Third Avenue
       New York, NY 10022

       Mrs. Dorothy Fax
       6405 Sixteenth Street N.W.
       Washington, DC 20012

       Theodore Presser Co.
       Bryn Mawr, PA 19010

FISCHER, WILLIAM SAMUEL (1935–)

Opera

Jack-Jack

SEE: Bote & Bock
    Associated Music Publishers, Inc.
    866 Third Avenue
    New York, NY 10022

    Ready Productions, Inc.
    500 West 122nd Street, Apt. 62
    New York, NY 10027

FLEMING, LARRY LEE (?)

Choral

Three about Jesus. 1. Every Time I Think about Jesus. 2. Give Me Jesus.
3. Ride On, King Jesus.
Augsburg Publishing House.

FLETCHER, JOHN (?)

Organ and Instruments

Suite. Organ, flute, clarinet, bassoon, violin, cello, and brass quartet.
Manuscript, ©1973.

SEE: John Fletcher
    Combermere School
    Barbados, West Indies

FLOYD, SAMUEL A., Jr. (?)

Book

The Great Lakes Experience, 1942–1945.
OCLC: 7502072.

University of Illinois

FOUNTAIN, PRIMOUS, III (1949–)
SEE: Belwin-Mills Pub. Corp.
    1776 Broadway
    New York, NY 10019

    Margun Music Inc.
    167 Dudley Road
    Newton Centre, MA 02159

Hindon Pub., Inc.
P.O. Box 470
Chapel Hill, NC 27514

FREEMAN, HARRY LAWRENCE (1870–1954)

Concerto

Viola and orchestra.

Opera

Voodoo.

U.S. Library of Congress

Orchestra

Fantasia and Dance. For violin and orchestra.

Matinee Suite. Three movements.

Symphonic Suite.

For Not Known

Divertimento.

If Thou Didst Love.

Images.

Whither.

FRIERSON, ANDREW (1927–)

SEE: Agape
Hope Publishing Company
380 South Main Place
Carol Stream, IL 60187

FURMAN, JAMES B. (1937–)

SEE: Hinshaw Music, Inc.
P.O. Box 470
Chapel Hill, NC 27514

Music 70 Music Pub.
170 North-East 33rd Street
Fort Lauderdale, FL 33334

Oxford University Press, Inc.
200 Madison Ave.
New York, NY 10016

Sam Fox Publishing Co., Inc.
73–941 Highway 111, Suite 11
Psalm Desert, CA 92260

G

GILLUM, RUTH HELEN (1907–)

SEE: J. Fischer & Bro.
       Belwin-Mills Pub. Corp.
       25 Deshon Drive
       Melville, NY 11746

GRAHAM, SHIRLEY (1908–77)

Opera

Tom-Tom. Three act.

Cleveland Public Library

For Not Known

I Promise.
Handy Bros. Music Co., Inc.

GRIDER, JOSEPH WILLIAM (?)

Orchestra

Suite.

For Not Known

Sonata.

H

HACKLEY, EMMA AZALEA SMITH (1867–1922)

Vocal

Carola. For voice with piano accompaniment.
Handy Bros. Music Co., Inc.

HAGAN, HELEN EUGENIA (1893–1964)

Concerto

C Minor. For piano and orchestra.

HAILSTORK, ADOLPHUS CUNNINGHAM, III (1941–)

Organ

Andante.
Manuscript, ©1967.

Prelude.
Manuscript, ©1967.

Indiana University

Suite. Four movements.
Hinshaw Music, Inc., ©1976.

University of New Mexico

Who Gazes at the Stars?
Manuscript, ©1978.

SEE: Edward B. Marks Music Corp.
1790 Broadway
New York, NY 10019

Hinshaw Music, Inc.
P.O. Box 470
Chapel Hill, NC 27514

HAIRSTON, JACQUELINE BUTLER (?)

Choral

Nowhere to Lay His Head. For four-part chorus of mixed voices a cappella
Edward B. Marks Music Corp.
Belwin-Mills Pub. Corp.

HAIRSTON, JESTER JOSEPH (1901–)

SEE:
Bourne Co.
Music Publishers
1212 Avenue of the Americas
New York, NY 10036

Hal Leonard Pub. Corp.
8112 West Bluemound Road
Milwaukee, WI 53213

Warner Bros. Music Publications
75 Rockefeller Plaza
New York NY 10019

HAKIM, TALIB RASUL (1940–) FORMERLY STEPHEN A. CHAMBERS

Various Instruments

Duo. For flute and clarinet.
Highgate Press, ©1963.
Galaxy Music Corp.

New York Public Library

HALL, FREDERICK DOUGLASS (1898–1964)

Book

Know Your Hymns Quiz.
Baker Book House, ©1972. OCLC: 2486970.

Akron–Summit County Public Library; Andrews University; Grand Rapids Baptist College and Seminary; Great Lakes Bible College; Iliff School of Theology;

Choral

Dry Bones. Negro spiritual. For four-part chorus of men's voices with piano accompaniment.
Rodeheaver Hall-Mack Co., ©1939.

Portland State College, Oregon

Negro Spirituals. Harmonized for quartet or chorus. Piano for rehearsal only. Book one: men's voices. Book two: women's voices. Book three: mixed voices.
Rodeheaver Hall-Mack Co., ©1938.

U.S. Library of Congress; University of Virginia

Orchestra

Negro Spirituals. Adapted to piano and orchestra. Three volumes.
Rodeheaver Hall-Mack Co., ©1939. OCLC: 6941129.

University of Virginia; College of William and Mary

Vocal

Good Night. Opus 4, no. 4. For medium voice with piano accompaniment. Words by Paul Laurence Dunbar.
Rodeheaver Co., ©1926.

Portland State College, Oregon

Mandy Lou. Opus 4, no. 3. For medium voice with piano accompaniment.
Rodeheaver Co., ©1926.

Portland State College, Oregon

Sing Songs of the Southland. Negro spirituals. For voice with piano accompaniment. No. 1. TTBB No. 2. SSA No. 3. SATB.
Rodeheaver Hall-Mack Co., ©1955.

Portland State College, Oregon

For Not Known

A Group of Unusual Negro Spirituals. With music.
Rodeheaver Co., ©1928.

Union Theological Seminary

Know Your Hymns.
W. A. Wilde, ©1944. OCLC: 3598622.

Abilene Christian University; Bethany Nazarene College; Southern Methodist University, Bridwell Library; Southwestern Baptist Theological Seminary

HANCOCK, EUGENE WILSON (1929–)

Choral

Jubilate (Psalm 100). Be Joyful in the Lord, All Ye Lands. For four-part chorus of mixed voices with organ accompaniment.
Anglo-American Music Publishers, ©1982.

Our Father in Heaven. For four-part chorus of mixed voices with soprano solo and piano accompaniment.
Augsburg Publishing House, ©1983.

Thirteen Spirituals. For chorus of equal voices in unison and two parts. Organ or unaccompanied.
1. Cavalry.
2. Go, Tell It on the Mountain.
3. I'm Troubled in Mind.
4. Let Us Break Bread Together.
5. Lord, I Want to Be a Christian.
6. My Soul's Been Anchored in the Lord.
7. O Redeemed.
8. Swing Low, Sweet Chariot.
9. There's a Star in the East.
10. This Little Light of Mine.
11. Wade in the Water.
12. Walk Together, Children.
13. Were You There?
H. W. Gray Inc., ©1973.
Belwin-Mills Pub. Corp.   OCLC: 967407

Cornell University; Southern Baptist Theological Seminary

Organ

An Organ Book of Spirituals. Two-staff.
Lorenz Pub. Co., ©1966.

Organ and Instruments

Suite in Three Movements. Strings, oboe, xylophone, and bass drum.
Manuscript, ©1967.

HANDY, WILLIAM CHRISTOPHER (1873–1958)

Book

Negro Authors and Composers of the United States.
Handy Brothers Music Co., Inc.

NUC Pre-1956 Imprints Volume 229, pp. 511–12.
Supplement, Volume 732, page 288.

For his works on Blues, Choral, Male quartets, Marches,
Orchestra, Ragtime, Spirituals, Vocal, et cetera.
OCLC: 2503302
9406751
6494705
6586729
7831920
6370977
5926613
356307
9452365
7426335
229819
8610287
5779082
4159313

SEE: Handy Bros. Music Co., Inc.
200 West 72nd St.
New York, NY 10023

Music, Printed and Manuscript in the James Weldon Johnson
Memorial Collection of Negro Arts and Letters. An annotated
catalog by Rae Linda Brown.
Garland Publishing, Inc.
New York and London, 1982.

HARE, MAUDE CUNEY (1874–1936)

Book

Negro Musicians and Their Music
The Associated Publishers, ©1936.
Da Capo Press, Inc., ©1974. OCLC: 885535, 835423, 2969426.

SEE: NUC Pre-1956 Imprints, V.231, p. 94 V.732, p. 392

OCLC

Vocal

Six Creole Folk Songs. For medium voice with piano accompaniment.
Original Creole and translated English text.
Carl Fischer, Inc. OCLC: 8659682, 8610294.

Boston Public Library; Brown University; Cleveland Public Library; Florida State University, Tallahassee; Free Library of Philadelphia; Harvard University; Indiana University; Johns Hopkins University; Joint University Libraries (Vanderbilt University, George Peabody Peabody College for Teachers, and Scarritt College); Newberry Library, Chicago

HARRIS, ETHEL RAMOS (1908–)

Choral

When I Reach the Other Side. For four-part chorus of mixed voices with piano accompaniment. Bongo drum accompaniment available separately. Words and music by E. R. Harris.
Volkwein Bros., Inc., ©1971.

Piano

Paquita Mia.
Volkwein Bros., Inc., ©1942.

Yolanda.
Volkwein Bros., Inc., ©1942.

HARRIS, HOWARD C., JR. (1940–)

SEE: Southern Music Co.
P.O. Box 329
San Antonio, TX 78292

HARRIS, MARGARET ROSEZARIAN (1943–)

Concerto

No. 2. For piano and orchestra.

For Not Known

Collage One.

Dear Love.

Grievin'.

Tonight's Goodbye.

HARRIS, ROBERT A. (1938–)

SEE: Joseph Boonin, Inc.
European American Music Distributors Corp.
195 Allwood
Clifton, NJ 07012

Mark Foster Music Co.
Box 4012
Champaign, IL 61820

HAYES, JOSEPH C. (1920–)

Organ

Praeludium.
Manuscript.

SEE: Joseph C. Hayes
17160 Kentucky
Detroit, MI 48221

HAYNES, EUGENE, JR. (1928–)

Orchestra

Symphony Fantasy. For piano and orchestra.

String Quartet

Title not known.

Vocal

Song cycle.

SEE: Eugene Haynes, Jr.
      Southern Illinois University
      East St. Louis Campus
      East St. Louis, IL 60101

HEBRON, J. HARVEY (?)

Violin

Sonata. Piano accompaniment.

HENRY, RAYMOND (1931–)

Organ

Two Hymn-tune Preludes. Eugen—King's Lynn.
Manuscript, ©1973.

SEE: Raymond Henry
      64 Gramercy Lane
      Willingboro, NJ 08046

HERBISON, JAMES W. (1947–)

Cello

Sonata. Number one.

Sonata. Number two.

Orchestra

Overture.

Trio

SEE: James W. Herbison
      34 Locust Avenue
      Hampton, VA 23661

HERBISON, JERALDINE SAUNDERS (1941–)

Cello

Fantasy in Three Moods.

Fugue. Unaccompanied.

Intermezzo. Piano accompaniment.

Sonata. Piano accompaniment.

Sonata. Unaccompanied.

Orchestra

Suite. For string orchestra, flute, and oboe.
Suite in C. For string orchestra.
Suite in F. For string orchestra.

Violin and Cello

Six Duos.

Vocal

Nine Art Songs. For voice with piano accompaniment.

SEE: Mrs. Jeraldine S. Herbison
34 Locust Avenue
Hampton, VA 23661

HEYWOOD, DONALD (1901–67)

For Not Known

Laz'rus. A descriptive Biblical story from "Blow, Gabriel, Blow."
Handy Bros. Music Co., Inc.

HICKS, L'ROY EDWARD (1931–)

SEE: Hope Publishing Co.
380 South Main Place
Carol Stream, IL 60187

HILL, EDWIN FRANCIS, JR. (?)

Violin

Jerusalem. Negro spiritual. Piano accompaniment.
Boston Public Library

HOLLAND, JUSTIN MINER (1819–1887)

59

Guitar Book

Holland's Comprehensive Method. 1874, revised 1876.
Oliver Ditson Co., ©1888, 1903, 1908.

Free Library of Philadelphia; New York Public Library; Oberlin College; State University of New York at Buffalo; Yale University

HOLT, NORA DOUGLAS (1895–1974)

Book

History of Negro Musicians.

String Quartet

Four.

For Not Known

Rhapsody on Negro Themes.

HUFFMAN, ETHEL BROWN (?)

Songs

Singable Songs for Tiny Tots. Rote songs for primary grades, set to music.
Shattering, ©1935.

J

JACKSON, EUGENE ALDAMA (1886–)

Choral

Go Down Moses.
H. W. Gray Co.
Belwin-Mills Pub. Corp.

For Not Known

Don't Be Weary, Traveler.

JACKSON, MARYLOU INDIA (?)

Choral

Negro Spirituals and Hymns. Arranged for chorus of women's voices and quartet. Fischer edition no. 6823.
J. Fischer & Bro., ©1935.
Belwin-Mills Pub. Corp.

New York Public Library; Union Theological Seminary, New York

JAMES, WILLIS LAURENCE (1909–66)

Choral

Negro Bell Carol. For four-part chorus of mixed voices a cappella.
Carl Fischer, Inc., ©1952. OCLC: 1839624.

Peabody Institute; Southern Illinois University

Oh, Po' Little Jesus. Negro spiritual. For four-part chorus of mixed voices with soprano solo a cappella.
G. Schirmer, Inc., ©1937. Publ. pl. no. 8170.

New York Public Library

Roun' de Glory Manger. Negro spiritual. For six-part chorus of mixed voices with soprano and tenor solos a cappella.
G. Schirmer, Inc., ©1937. Publ. pl. no. 37886.

JENKINS, EDMUND THORTON (1894–1926)

Cello ·

Sonata in A Minor.

Orchestra

Charlestonia. Negro Folk Rhapsody.

Rapsodie Spirituelle. Negro Folk Rhapsody No. 2.

Organ

Prélude Religieuse.

For Not Known

African War Dance.

Three Art Songs. Words by Lady Lindsay.

JESSYE, EVA ALBERTA (1895–)

Choral

Simon the Fisherman. A Negro song. For chorus of mixed voices with narrators.
C. C. Birchard & Co.
Summy-Birchard Co.

Folk Drama

Chronicle of Job.

Oratorio

Paradise Lost And Regained. For chorus, two narrators, and organ. John Milton text.

Vocal

My Spirituals. For voice with piano accompaniment.

Illustrated by Millar of the Roland Co., edited by Gordon Whyte and Hugo Frey.
Robbins-Engel Music Corp., ©1927.

Cleveland Public Library; Duke University; Free Library of Philadelphia; New York Public Library; U.S. Library of Congress; University of California, Berkeley; University of California, Los Angeles; University of Idaho; University of Pennsylvania; University of Virginia; Yale University, James Weldon Johnson Memorial Collection

JOHNS, ALTONA TREET (1904–77)

Songs

Finger Fun with Songs to Be Sung. Verses by Vivian Flagg McBrier.
Handy Bros. Music Co., Inc., ©1949.

Howard University

Play Songs of the Deep South. Piano accompaniment. Illustrations by James A. Porter.
The Associated Publishers Inc., ©1944.

Boston Public Library; Cleveland Public Library; Cornell University; Free Library of Philadelphia; Girard College; Hampton Institute; Library Association of Portland, Oregon; Ohio State University; Oregon State Library; Pennsylvania State University; Philadelphia Board of Public Education, Pedagogical Library; Spokane Public Library; State University of New York at Buffalo; U.S. Library of Congress; University of Chicago; University of Georgia; University of North Carolina at Greensboro; University of Utah; University of Virginia; Washington State Library; West Chester State College; Yale University, James Weldon Johnson Memorial Collection

JOHNSON, BESSIE VIOLA (1878–)

Cantata

Ode to Faith. For chorus, solos, and orchestra.
Reproduced from manuscript.

New York Public Library

JOHNSON, FRANCIS (1792–1844)

Flute

Recognition March of the Inderpendence of Haiti. Piano accompaniment.

G. Willig, © circa 1820.

U.S. Library of Congress

JOHNSON, HALL (1888–1970)

Cantata

Son of Man.

Choral

Ain't Got Time to Die. Negro spiritual. For four-part chorus of mixed voices with tenor solo a cappella. Octavo no. 10301.
G. Schirmer, Inc., ©1955.

Peabody Institute; Southern Illinois University

Cert'y Lord. For four-part chorus of mixed voices with tenor and bass solos a cappella.
Carl Fischer, Inc., ©1952.

Southern Illinois University

Ride On King Jesus, King Of Kings. Negro spiritual. For four-part chorus of mixed voices with tenor solo a cappella.
Carl Fischer, Inc.

Peabody Institute

Spiritual Moods. Based on traditional Negro melodies. For chorus of men's voices with orchestra accompaniment.

Spiritual Moods No. 2. For chorus of men's voices with orchestra accompaniment. 1. City Called Heaven. 2. I Want to Be Ready. 3. In Bright Mansions Above. 4. Ride On, King Jesus! 5. Trampin'. 6. You May Bury Me in de Eas'.
Photocopy of holograph, ©1955.

New York Public Library

Steal Away. Negro spiritual. For four-part chorus of men's voices a cappella.
Carl Fischer, Inc., ©1935.

Southern Illinois University, Edwardsville Campus

'Way Up in Heaven. Negro spiritual. For four-part chorus of mixed voices with piano accompaniment.

Robbins Music Corp., ©1930.
Big 3 Music Corp.

Operetta

Coophered.

Fi-Yer.

Orchestra

Festival March. To the black soldiers of America.

Norfolk. Five movements.

Suite. For string orchestra. Five movements.

String Quartet

G Major. Four movements.

Violin

Sonata in A Minor.

Vocal

The Green Pastures Spirituals. Arranged for voice with piano accompaniment.
Carl Fischer, Inc., ©1930.

Ride On King Jesus, King Of Kings. Negro spiritual. For voice with piano accompaniment.
Carl Fischer, Inc., ©1951. Publ. pl. no. 30885–5.

Thirty Negro Spirituals. Arranged for voice with piano accompaniment.
G. Schirmer, Inc., ©1949.

30 Negro Spirituals. Arranged for voice with piano accompaniment. English words. Für Gesang und Klavier. Pelikan Edition 783. Preface in German and French.
Zurich: Musikverlag Zum Pelikan, ©1949.

Boston Public Library

Three Negro Spirituals. For voice with piano accompaniment. 1. His Name So Sweet. 2. Hold On. 3. Jesus, Lay Your Head in de Winder. Robbins Music Corp., ©1930–34.
Big 3 Music Corp.

Boston Public Library

JOHNSON, JOHN RASAMOND (1873–1954)

Choral

Utica Jubilee Singers Spirituals. For four-part chorus of men's voices with piano accompaniment.
Oliver Ditson Co., ©1930.

Boston Public Library; Fisk University; Harvard University; Howard University; Library Association of Portland, Oregon; New York Public Library; New York University, Washington Square Library; Newberry Library, Chicago; University of Chicago

Piano

African Drum Dance No. 1.
London: J. Curwen & Sons Ltd., ©1928.

Yale University, James Weldon Johnson Memorial Collection

Violin

Nobody Knows the Trouble I See. Arrangement by J. R. Johnson transcribed with piano accompaniment by Maud Powell.
Oliver Ditson Co., ©1921.

Library Association of Portland, Oregon

Vocal

Album of Negro Spirituals. Newly adapted and arranged for soprano with piano accompaniment.
Edward B. Marks Music Corp., ©1940.

U.S. Library of Congress; University of Oregon

The Awakening. For voice with piano accompaniment. Words by James Weldon Johnson.
G. Ricordi & Co., ©1913.

New York Public Library; Yale University, James Weldon Johnson Memori Collection

De Chain Gang. For eight-part chorus of men's voices with piano accompaniment. Musical episode based on work songs of the Southland with descriptive continuity and light effects.
Handy Bros. Music Co., Inc., ©1938

Stanford University Memorial Library of Music; U.S. Library of Congress

A Collection of Songs. For voice with piano accompaniment. 1. De Little Pickaninn'y Gone to Sleep. 2. Nobody Knows the Trouble I See. 3. Walk Together Children.
Oliver Ditson Co., ©1910–17.

Boston Public Library

I Told My Love To the Roses. For high voice with piano accompaniment. Poem by J. A. Middleton.
G. Schirmer, Inc., ©1916.

New York Public Library

Life Is a Game of Checkers. For voice and piano accompaniment.
J. W. Stern & Co., ©1908.

New York Public Library; Yale University, James Weldon Johnson Memorial Collection

Lit' Gal. For voice with piano accompaniment. Words by Paul Lawrence Dunbar.
J. W. Stern & Co., ©1902.

New York Public Library; Yale University, James Weldon Johnson Memorial Collection

Morning, Noon and Night. For high voice with piano accompaniment. Words by James Weldon Johnson.
G. Schirmer, Inc., ©1916.

New York Public Library; Yale University, James Weldon Johnson Memorial Collection

Nobody the Trouble I See. For high voice—low voice with piano accompaniment.
Oliver Ditson Co., ©1921.

New York Public Library; Yale University, James Weldon Johnson Memorial Collection

Since You Went Away. For voice with piano accompaniment. Words by James Weldon Johnson.
G. Ricordi & Co., ©1913.

New York Public Library; Yale University, James Weldon Johnson Memorial Collection
Sixteen New Spirituals. Arranged and adapted for voice with piano accompaniment.
Handy Bros. Music Co., Inc., ©1939.

Brown University; Cleveland Public Library; Duke University; Oregon State Library; Stanford University Memorial Library of Music; U.S. Library of Congress

Sweet Rain. An Oriental love song. For voice with piano accompaniment. Words and music by J. R. Johnson.
Oliver Diston Co., ©1947.

Ten Choice Negro Folk Songs. For voice with piano accompaniment. H. Dacre, J. R. Johnson, and C. Smith.
Globe Music Co., ©1901.

University of Oklahoma

Three Questions. A ballad. For voice with piano accompaniment. Poem by James Weldon Johnson.
Harold Flammer, Inc., ©1917.

New York Public Library; Ohio State University

K

KAY, ULYSSES SIMPSON (1917–)

SEE: Associated Music Pub., Inc.
866 Third Avenue
New York, NY 10022

Belwin-Mills Pub. Corp.
1776 Broadway
New York, NY 10019

C. F. Peters Corp.
373 Park Avenue South
New York, NY 10016

Duchess Music Corp.
221 Park Avenue South
New York, NY 10016

Pembroke Music Co., Inc.
Carl Fischer, Inc.
56–62 Cooper Square
New York, NY 10003

Peer-Southern Organization
1740 Broadway
New York, NY 10019

KENNEDY, MATTHEW W. (1921–)

Choral

Two Spirituals. Ev'ry Time I Feel the Spirit. Steal Away to Jesus. For four-part chorus of mixed voices.
Abingdon Press.

KERR, THOMAS HENDERSON, JR. (1915–)

Organ

Arietta (Sumco 5063).

Suite Sebastian.
Manuscript.

Thanksgiving.
Manuscript, ©1969.

Variations On a Merry Christmas Tune, "Good King Wenceslas."
Manuscript, ©1951.

SEE: Thomas H. Kerr, Jr.
      1845 Laurel Ridge Dr
      Parkton, MD 21120

KILLINGSWORTH, JOHN DEKOVEN (1898–1982)

Book

Form and Analysis. ©1940.

KING, BETTY JACKSON (1928–)

Ballet

The Kids in School with Me.

Cantata

Simon of Cyrene.

Choral

Requiem.

Opera

My Servant Job.

Oratorio

Saul of Tarsus.

Organ

Nuptial Suite. 1. Processional. 2. Nuptial Song. 3. Recessional.

Piano

Fantastic Mirror.

Four Season Sketches. 1. Spring Intermezzo. 2. Summer Interlude. 3. Autumn Dance. 4. Winter Holiday.

Mother Goose Parade.

Vocal

Dawn.

God Shall Wipe Away All Tears.

A Lover's Plea.

L

LAMBERT, LUCIEN LEON GUILLAUME (1858–1945)

Vocal

Le Spahi. Piano accompaniment. French text.

New York Public Library

For Not Known

La Juive.

L'Américaine.

Le Niagara.

LAMOTHE, LUDOVIC (1882–1953)

Piano

Papillons Noirs. Valse lente. Bruxelles.
Mahilon & Co., ©1910. Publ. pl. no. M. & Co. 275.

New York Public Library

Valses, Dances Espancles. Scènes de carnal, et autres.
Port-au-Prince, Haiti, ©1955.

Duke University; New York Public Library; Oregon State Library, Salem; U.S. Library of Congress; University of Florida, Gainesville; University of Miami, Coral Gables; University of Texas, Austin

LATEEF, YUSEF ABDUL (1920–), FORMERLY WILLIAM "BILL" EVANS

Organ

Fantasia.
Manuscript.

72

SEE: c/o Alnur Music
   RFD No. 2
   Baker Road
   Amherst, MA 01002

OCLC

LAVERGNE, PATRICK (1955–)

String Bass

Three Movements. Unaccompanied.

Violin

Elegy.

SEE: Patrick LaVergne
   P.O. Box 1201
   Opelousas, LA 70570

LAWRENCE, WILLIAM (1897–1966)

String Quartet

Three Negro Spirituals.

For Not Known

Aframerica Rhapsodie No. 1.

Bambara.

Let Us Break Bread Together on Our Knees. Negro spiritual.
McLaughlin & Reilly Co., ©1945.
Summy-Birchard Co.

Library Association of Portland, Oregon

Rhapsodie Africaine.

LAYTON, JOHN TURNER, SR. (1841–1916)

Book

Hymnal. African Methodist Episcopal.

LEON, TANIA JUSTINA (1944–)

Ballet

Tones. Three Movements.

Orchestra

Haiku.

LEWIS, FREDERICK ELLIOT (1846–?)

Piano

Fantasia. Opus 3.

LLOYD, CHARLES, JR. (1948–)

Piano

Sonatina.

Vocal

Eight Spirituals.

SEE: Charles Lloyd, Jr.
       37 South King Road
       Holland, OH 43528

LOGAN, WENDELL MORRIS (1940–)

SEE: Wendell M. Logan
       167 South Pleasant Street
       Oberlin, OH 44704

LOVINGGOOD, PENMAN, SR. (1895–)

Book

Famous Modern Negro Musicians.
Press Forum Co., ©1921.
Da Capo Press, ©1978.

New York Public Library; U.S. Library of Congress; University of New Mexico

Opera

Menelik. Evangeline and Gabriel.

Vocal

I Am Sure, My Love. For voice with piano accompaniment. Words by Zella.

New York Public Library

M

MCCARTY, VICTOR EUGENE (1821–CIRCA 1890)

Piano

Fleurs de Salon. La Caprifolia—L' Azalea.

Tulane University, Howard-Tilton Library; University of New Orleans, Marcus B. Christian Collection of the Earl Long Library

MCDANIEL, WILLIAM FOSTER (1940–)

Piano

Sonata.

Woodwind

Quintet.

MCLIN, LENA JOHNSON (1928–)

SEE: Edward B. Marks Music Corp.
1790 Broadway
New York, NY 10019

Neil A. Kjos Music Co.
4382 Jutland Drive
San Diego, CA 92117

Pro Art Publication Inc.
Belwin-Mills Pub. Corp.
25 Deshon Drive
Melville, NY 11746

MCSWAIN, AUGUSTA GERALDINE (1917–)

Piano

Six Pieces.

MARCUS, WADE (?)

Violin

A Moorish Sonata. Piano accompaniment.

MARGETSON, EDWARD HENRY (1891–1962)

Cello

Ballade, Valse, Serenade.

Orchestra

Ronda Caprice.

For Not Known

Echoes of the Caribbean.

SEE: Boston Music Co.
116–122 Boylston Street
Boston, MA 02116

Galaxy Music Corp.
131 West 86th Street, Ninth floor
New York, NY 10024

J. Fischer & Bro.
H. W. Gray Co., Inc.
Belwin-Mills Pub. Corp.
25 Deshon Drive
Melville, NY 11746

MAULTSBY, PORTIA KATRENIA (1947–)

SEE: OCLC

MAYES, ROBERT M. (1910–)

Studies and Exercises

Oboe Passages Extracted from the Works of Famous Composers. By R.
M. Mayes.
Belwin Inc. OCLC: 7857718.

Memphis State University; San Francisco State University; University of Arizona; University of Texas, Austin; Wartburg College, Waverly

MELLS, HERBERT FRANKLIN (1909–53)

Choral

Behold. For four-part chorus of mixed voices a cappella.
Handy Bros. Co., Inc., ©1949.

A Christmas Lullaby. For four-part chorus of mixed voices with soprano and alto solos a cappella.
Handy Bros. Music Co., Inc., ©1959.

Come On, Sinner. For four-part chorus of mixed voices a cappella.
Handy Bros. Music Co., Inc., ©1949.

Go Tell It on the Mountain. For four-part chorus of mixed voices a cappella.
Handy Bros. Co., Inc., ©1949.

My Soul's Been Anchored in the Lord. For four-part chorus of mixed voices with soprano solo a cappella.
Handy Bros. Co., Inc., ©1948.

The Preaching of the Elders. For four-part chorus of men's voices a cappella.
Handy Bros. Co., Inc., ©1949.

Orchestra

Motherless Child. Negro spiritual. A symphonic poem.
Black-line print from manuscript copy, ©1944.

U.S. Library of Congress

Quintet

A Minor. B-flat clarinet, two violins, viola, and cello. Facsimile of manuscript.

University of Iowa

For Not Known

Burdened Chile.

Ten Concertized Arrangements.
Handy Bros. Co., Inc.

MERRIFIELD, NORMAN LAVELLE (1906–)

Choral

Down by the Rivuhside. Negro spiritual. For four-part chorus of mixed voices a cappella.
Neil A. Kjos Music Co., ©1958. OCLC: 1413459.

Southern Illinois University

Remember O Lord. For four-part chorus of mixed voices with piano or organ accompaniment.
Boston Music Co., ©1964. OCLC: 1413474.

Southern Illinois University

SEE: Handy Bros. Music Co., Inc.
200 West 72nd Street
New York, NY 10023

Richmond Music Press
P.O. Box 465
Richmond, IN 47374

MILLER, JAMES M. (1907–70)

Choral

Daniel.

Didn't My Lord Deliver Daniel?

I Am Seeking for a City.

I Wanna Be Ready.

You Gonna Reap.

For Not Known

Please Don't Drive Me Away.

So Fades the Lovely Blooming Flow'r.

MILLER, LESTER (?)

Band

Onedolin. March.

MOFFATT, RICHARD CULLEN (1927–82)

Cantata

As It Began to Dawn. (Easter.)

The Comforter.

Jerusalem.

Choral

Alleluia! For four-part chorus of mixed voices.

Alleluia, Let Us Sing! For four-part chorus of mixed voices.

I Will Lift Up Mine Eyes unto the Hills. For four-part chorus of mixed voices.

In The Beginning Was the Word. For four-part chorus of mixed voices.

Oh, Rest in the Lord. For four-part chorus of mixed voices. An arrangement of a Felix Mendelssohn-Bartholdy work.

Opera

Cinderella.

Rumpelstiltskin.

A Song for Ruby-Jo. One-act opera.

Piano

Concerto.

Preludes.

Trio.

Violin

Sonata.

For Not Known

Emily Dickinson Songs.

O Divine Master.

When Lilacs Last in the Dooryard Bloom'd.

MONTAGUE, J. HAROLD (1906–50)

Choral

Joshua Fit de Battle ob Jerico. For four-part chorus of mixed voices with baritone solo a cappella.
M. Witmark & Sons, ©1935. Publ. pl. no. 2302979.
Warner Bros. Pub., Inc. OCLC: 2302979.

Hebrew Union College

MOORE, CARMEN LEROY (1936–)

Choral

Follow Light. For four-part chorus of mixed voices, two soprano solos, with percussion and double bass. In memory of Texana Paige Franklin. Manuscript, ©1977.

SEE: Peer-Southern Organization
1740 Broadway
New York, NY 10019

MOORE, DOROTHY RUDD (1940–)

SEE: American Composers Alliance
170 West 74th Street
New York, NY 10023

Rudmor Pub. Co.
33 Riverside Drive
New York, NY 10023

MOORE, KERMIT (1929–)

Choral

Many Thousand Gone.

Concerto

Timpani and orchestra.

Vocal

Four Areas. Adapted for soprano and symphony orchestra.

SEE: Kermit Moore
      33 Riverside Drive
      New York, NY 10023

MOORE, UNDINE SMITH (1904–)

Choral

Let Us Make Man in Our Own Image. For four-part chorus of mixed voices with soprano solo a cappella.
M. Witmark & Sons, ©1960.
Warner Bros. Pub. Inc.

Organ

Variation on "Nettleton."
Manuscript

SEE: Augsburgh Publishing House
      426 South Fifth Street
      Minneapolis, MN 55415

      H. W. Gray Co., Inc.
      Belwin-Mills Pub. Corp.
      25 Deshon Drive
      Melville, NY 11746

      M. Witmark & Sons
      Warner Bros Publications, Inc.
      75 Rockefeller Plaza
      New York, NY 10019

MORGAN, WILLIAM ASTOR (1890–?), PSEUDONYM: JEAN STOR

Anthems

Bibical Choral Series.
    Be Still and Know (Forty-sixth Psalm).
    God Is Our Refuge (Forty-sixth Psalm).
    One Hundred Thirty-seventh Psalm.
    The Kingdoms of Our Lord (Revelation 22:15–17).
    The Lord's Prayer.
    The Water of Life (Revelation 22:1–7).
    These Are They (Revelation 7:11–17).
Handy Bros. Music Co., Inc.

Operetta

Jericho's Walls. Folk play.

Orchestra

Adagio. Opus 74. In memory of our friend, Franklin Delano Roosevelt. Black-line print from manuscript copy. ©1945.

U.S. Library of Congress

Vocal

I Want Jesus to Walk with Me. Negro spiritual. Voice with piano accompaniment.
Handy Bros. Music Co., Inc., ©1935.

New York Public Library

For Not Known

This Is a Sin-trying World.
Handy Bros. Music Co., Inc.

MORRISON, GEORGE SUMNER, SR. (1891–1974)

Musical Play

Roxana Steps Out. Written by Carmen Gerace and G. Morrison, Sr. Manuscript, ©1943.

U.S. Library of Congress

Violin

Five Solos. Piano accompaniment.
Handy Bros. Music Co., Inc., ©1947.

MOSELEY, JAMES ORVILLE BROWN (1909–)

Concerto

Piano and Orchestra. Three movements.

Opera

How Long the Road.

Orchestra

Fort McHenry. Tone poem.

Suite. Five movements. For string orchestra.

Symphony in A.

For Not Known

Lento and Toccata.

MUNDY, JAMES AHLYN (1886–1978)

For Not Known

Ethiopia.

N

NICKERSON, CAMILLE LUCIE (1887 OR '88–1982)

Choral

Gué-Gué Solingaié. Creole folk lullaby. For four-part chorus of mixed voices a cappella.
Leeds Music Corp., ©1948.
Belwin-Mills Pub. Co.

Vocal

Creole Folk Songs. For voice.
1. Dance, Baby, Dance.
2. Dear, I Love You So.
3. Go to Sleep.
4. Lizette, My Dearest One.
5. Mister Banjo.
Arranged by C. W. Nickerson. Creole and English words.
Boston Music Co., ©1942.

University of Texas, Austin

SEE: Sam Fox Publishing Co., Inc.
73–941 Highway 111, Suite 11
Psalm Desert, CA 92260

NKETIA, JOSEPH HANSON KWABENA (1921–)

Vocal

Akanfoo Nnwom Bi Nsem. For voice. Akan folk song. Akan language.
Oxford University Press, ©1955.

University of California, Los Angeles

NORMAN, JEANNETTE LATIMER (?)

Piano

A Day in the Life of a Child. Seven episodes in easy style. Carl Fischer, Inc., ©1924.

O

OWENS, BANKSTON (?)

SEE: J. A. Parks Music Corp.
Neil A. Kjos Music Co.
4382 Jutland Drive
San Diego, CA 92117

OWENS, ROBERT (1925–)

Opera

Orchestra

Vocal

Border line. Song cycle. Opus 24. For voice and piano. Poems of Langston Hughes.
Munich: Orlando-Musikverlag, ©1970.

Desire. Song cycle. For tenor voice with piano accompaniment. Words by Langston Hughes
Munich: Orlando-Musikverlag.

Yale University, James Weldon Johnson Memorial Collection

In time of silver rain. Song cycle. For voice and piano. Words by Langston Hughes.
Munich: Orlando-Musikverlag.

Tearless. For voice and piano. Lyrics by Langston Hughes. Photocopy.

Catalog

P

PARKER, KAYE (?)

For Not Known

Hold On.
Handy Bros. Music Co., Inc.

Wade in de Water.
Handy Bros. Music Co., Inc.

PARKER, REGINALD NATHANIEL, SR. (1929–70)

SEE: Handy Bros. Music Co., Inc.
200 West 72nd Street
New York, NY 10023

PARKS, GORDON ALEXANDER (1912–)

Orchestra

Symphonic Sets. Piano and orchestra.

PERKINSON, COLERIDGE-TAYLOR (1932–)

SEE: Tosci Music Corp.
Belwin-Mills Pub. Corp.
25 Deshon Drive
Melville, NY 11746

PERRY, JULIA AMANDA (1927–79)

Cantata

Chicago. For chorus, baritone solo, narrator, and two pianos. Revised January 1950. Words by Carl Sandburg.
Film copy; negative—positive.

Newberry Library, Chicago; University of Chicago

Choral

Be Merciful unto Me, O God. For chorus of mixed voices, soprano, and bass solos with organ accompaniment. Words from Psalm 57:1, 2.
Galaxy Music Corp.

Carillon Heigh-Ho. For four-part chorus of mixed voices a cappella.
Carl Fischer, Inc., ©1947.

Boston Public Library

Our Thanks to Thee. For chorus of mixed voices with contralto solo. Piano or organ accompaniment. An anthem for Thanksgiving or general use.
Galaxy Music Corp., ©1962.

Ye Who Seek The Truth. For four-part chorus of mixed voices with tenor solo. Organ accompaniment.
Galaxy Music Corp., ©1962.

Southern Illinois University

Concerto

Violin and Orchestra.
Carl Fischer, Inc.

Orchestra

Contretemps.

A Simple Symphony. One movement.

Violin

Sonata.

Vocal

How Beautiful Are the Feet. For voice with piano accompaniment.

New York Public Library

Lord! What Shall I Do? For soprano with piano accompaniment.
McLaughlin & Reilly Co.
Summy-Birchard Co.

Stabat Mater. Arranged for contralto and string quartet or string orchestra.

89

Peer-Southern Organization Publ. pl. no. 215–25.

Boston Public Library; Florida State University; Free Library of Philadelphia; Louisiana State University; New York Public Library; Southern Illinois University; University of Kansas, Lawrence

For Not Known

By the Sea.
Galaxy Music Corp.

PHILLIPS, ARTHUR A. (1918–)

Organ

Choral, Variations and Fugue in C Minor.
Manuscript, ©1971.

SEE: Arthur A. Phillips
537 West 141 Street
New York, NY 10031

PITTMAN, EVELYN LA RUE (1910–)

Choral

I Love the Springtime. For chorus of mixed voices with piano accompaniment.
Evelyn Pittman.

Oklahoma Is My Home. For chorus of mixed voices.
Manuscript.

Rocka Mah Soul. Negro spiritual. For five-part chorus of mixed voices with baritone solo a cappella.
Carl Fischer, Inc., ©1952. OCLC: 1827179.

Southern Illinois University; Yale University, James Weldon Johnson Memorial Collection.

Trampin'. For four-part chorus of mixed voices a cappella.
Jack Spratt Music Co., ©1961.

We Love America. For chorus of mixed voices.
Evelyn Pittman, ©1951.

Music Drama

Freedom Child.
Manuscript, ©1977.

Jim Noble.
Manuscript, ©1977.

Opera

Cousin Esther.
Manuscript, ©1954. Revised, 1956.

Songs

Rich Heritage. Songs about American Negro heroes. Elementary level.
Voice with piano accompaniment.
Harlow Pub. Corp., ©1944. Revised, 1968.

New York Public Library, Schomburg Collection; Northwestern University; Yale University, James Weldon Johnson Memorial Collection

PRICE, FLORENCE BEATRICE SMITH (1898–1953)

Band

Three Little Negro Dances. Arranged for band by Eric Leidzen.
Theodore Presser Co., ©1939.

Choral

Heav'n Bound Soldier. Arranged for three-part chorus of women's voices. Piano accompaniment.
Handy Bros. Music Co., Inc., ©1949.

The Moon Bridge. For chorus of women's voices.
Remick Music Corp., ©1950.
Warner Bros Pub. Inc.

Nature's Magic. For chorus of women's voices. Words by Mary Rolofson Gamble.
Clayton F. Summy Co.
Summy-Birchard Co.

New Moon. For chorus of women's voices with optional soprano obligato and four-hands piano accompaniment.

Remick Music Corp.
Warner Bros. Pub. Inc.

Song for Snow. For chorus of mixed voices with piano accompaniment.
Carl Fischer, Inc., ©1957.

Witch of the Meadow. For three-part chorus of women's voices. Words
by Mary Rolofson Gamble.
Remick Music Corp.
Warner Bros. Pub. Inc.

Concerto

In D Major. For violin and orchestra.

In D Minor. For piano and orchestra.
Manuscript, ©1934.

In F Minor. For piano and orchestra.
Manuscript, ©1934.

One movement. For piano and orchestra.

Orchestra

Colonial Dance Symphony.

Concert Overture No. 1. Based on Negro spirituals.

Concert Overture No. 2. Based on Negro spirituals.

Dances in the Canebrakes. Suite.
Belwin-Mills Pub. Corp.

Ethiopia's Shadow in America.
Manuscript, ©1932.

Mississippi River. Symphony.
Manuscript.

The Oak. A tone poem.

Symphony in D Minor. Four movements.
Manuscript.

Symphony in E Minor. Four movements.

Symphony In G Minor.
Manuscript.

Symphony No. 3 In C Minor. Four movements.
Manuscript, ©1940.

Yale University, James Weldon Johnson Memorial Collection

Organ

Adoration.
Lorenz Pub. Co.

Evening Song.

In Quiet Mood.
Galaxy Music Corp., ©1951. OCLC: 1397941.

Governors State University; Southern University

Offertory.
Lorenze Pub. Co.

Passacaglia and Fugue.
Manuscript.

Sonata No. 1.
Manuscript.

Suite No. 1.

Variation on a Folk Song.

Piano

At the Cotton Gin.
G. Schirmer, Inc.

Bright Eyes.
Theodore Presser Co., ©1937.

Cabin Song.
Theodore Presser Co., ©1937.

Cotton Dance.
Carl Fischer, Inc., ©1942.

Cotton Dance. In: *Oxford Piano Course*, Fifth Book.
Oxford University Press.

Dances in the Canebrakes. Based on authentic Negro rhythms.

Five Easy Compositions.
McKinley Music Co., ©1928. Publ. pl. no. 2241.

The Goblin and the Mosquito.
Clayton F. Summy Co., ©1951.
Summy-Birchard Co.

Levee Dance.
Theodore Presser Co., ©1937.

A Morning Sunbeam.
Theodore Presser Co., ©1937.

Nobody Knows the Trouble I See.
Theodore Presser Co., ©1938.

The Old Boatman.
Clayton F. Summy Co., ©1951.
Summy-Birchard Co.

Pieces We Like To Play. 1. The Butterfly. 2. The Gnat and the Bee.
3. The Rose.
Carl Fischer, Inc., ©1936.

A Sachem's Pipe.
Carl Fischer, Inc. ©1935.

The Sea Swallow.
Clayton F. Summy Co., ©1951.
Summy-Birchard Co.

Sonata in E Minor.
©1932.

Tecumseh.
Carl Fischer, Inc., ©1935.

Three Little Negro Dances. 1. Hoe Cake. 2. Rabbit Foot. 3. Ticklin'
Toes.
Theodore Presser Co., ©1933.

Were You There When They Crucified My Lord?
Carl Fischer, Inc., ©1942.

Were You There When They Crucified My Lord? In: *Oxford Piano
Course*, Fifth Book.
Oxford University Press.

The Zephyr (El Cafiro). A Mexican folk song. Arranged for piano by
F. B. Price.
McKinley Music Co., ©1928.

Piano, Duet

Annie Laurie.
McKinley Music Co., ©1947.

The Goblin and the Mosquito.
Clayton F. Summy Co., ©1951.
Summy-Birchard Co.

Silent Night.
McKinley Music Co.

Three Little Negro Dances.
Theodore Presser Co., ©1949.

Violin

By Candlelight. Piano accompaniment.
McKinley Music Co.

The Deserted Garden. Piano accompaniment.
Theodore Presser Co., ©1933.

Mellow Twilight.
McKinley Music Co.

Playful Rondo.
McKinley Music Co.

Vocal

An April Day. For voice. Words by Joseph F. Cotter.
Handy Bros. Music Co., Inc., ©1949.

The Moon Bridge. For chorus of women's voices.
Remick Music Corp., ©1950.
Warner Bros. Pub., Inc.

My Soul's Been Anchored in de Lord. For voice and piano—for voice
and orchestra.
Carl Fischer, Inc., ©1937.

Night. For voice and piano. Words by Louise C. Wallace.
Edward B. Marks Music Corp., ©1946.

Out of the South Blew a Wind. For voice and piano. Words by Fanny Carter.
Edwards B. Marks Music Corp., ©1946.

Songs to the Dark Virgin. For voice with piano accompaniment. Words by Langston Hughes.
G. Schirmer, Inc., ©1941.

University of Illinois; Yale University, James Weldon Johnson Memorial Collection

Two Traditional Negro Spirituals. For voice with piano accompaniment. 1. I'm Bound for the Kingdom. 2. I'm Workin' on My Buildin'.
Handy Bros. Music Co., Inc., ©1949.

For Not Known

Fantasie No. 4.

The Waterfall.
McKinley Music Co.

PRICE, JOHN ELWOOD (1935–)

Organ

Meditation for April Third.
Manuscript, ©1956.

Piece.
Manuscript, ©1969.

SEE: Slave Ship Press
        5030 Northwest Seventh Avenue
        Miami, FL 33127

R

REECE, DONALD CORTEZ (1910–74)

Piano

Studies.

Suite.

For Not Known

Sonata.

SEE: Hinshaw Music, Inc.
P.O. Box 470
Chapel Hill, NC 27514

Summy-Birchard Co.
Box CN 27
Princeton, NJ 08540

RIVERS, CLARENCE JOSEPH (1931–)

OCLC

SEE: Stimuli Inc.
15 West Sixth Street
Cincinnati, OH 45202

ROBERTS, HOWARD ALFRED (1924–)

SEE: Lawson-Gould Music Pub., Inc.
866 Third Avenue
New York, NY 10022

ROBINSON, ALPHONSE (1910–)

Choral

Soliloquy to a Martyred Hero. A trilogy. Opus 22. For four-part chorus of mixed voices with full orchestra accompaniment. Written in cooperation with the late Betty McConnell Brewster of Denver, Colorado. Manuscript, ©1978.

SEE: Alphonse Robinson
         2744 Gaylord Street
         Denver, CO 80205

ROBINSON, JOSEPHUS (?)

SEE: Josephus Robinson
         7704 South Honore Street
         Chicago, IL 60620

ROLDAN, AMADEO (1900–1939)

Ballet

El Milagro De Aπaquillé, Misterio Africano Cuban. Choreographic mystery in one act.

In Rebambaramba, Africano Cuban. One act.

Cello

Two Popular Cuban Songs. Piano accompaniment.
Peer-Southern Organization.

New York Public Library

Choral

Motivos de Song Negro Bembón, Ayé Me Dijeron Negro. For four-part chorus of mixed voices with vocal syllables.
New Music, quarterly of modern composition, vol. 7, no. 2.

Boston Public Library; Library Association of Portland, Oregon; New York Public Library; U.S. Library of Congress; University of Colorado; University of Illinois; University of North Carolina, Greensboro; Yale University

Orchestra

Himno Del A.B.C. Treble voices ad. lib.
Peer-Southern Organization.

La Muerte Alegre Música Incidental.
Peer-Southern Organization.

Overture on Cuban Folk Themes.
Peer-Southern Organization.

Suite. From ballet: *La Rebambaramba.*
Carl Fischer, Inc.

Three Little Poems.
Carl Fischer, Inc.

Piano

The Diablito Dances. (Juvenile.)
M P2200.
Carl Fischer, Inc., ©1941.

University of Illinois

Mulato.
Peer-Southern Organization

Negro Baby's Lullaby. (Saminsky-Freed). ME. P2199.
Carl Fischer, Inc.

Vocal

Danza Negra. For high voice and seven instruments. Text by F. Pales Mato.
Peer-Southern Organization.

Motivos De Son: Ochos Canciones Cubanas para canto y Pequena Orquesta. Eight Cuban songs. For high voice and small orchestra. Spanish words. 1. Ayé Me Dijeron Negro. 2. Bucate Plato. 3. Mi Chiquita. 4. Mulata. 5. Negro Bembón. 6. Si Tu Su Piera. 7. Sigue. 8. Tu No Sabe Ingle. New Music Orchestra Series. No. 16.
New Music, ©1935–36.

Harvard University; Stanford University; U.S. Library of Congress; University of Illinois; University of Iowa; Yale University

ROXBURY, RONALD MARLE (1946–)

SEE: Walton Music Corp.
Hal Leonard Pub. Corp.
8112 West Bluemound Road
Milwaukee, WI 53213

RYDER, NOAH FRANCIS (1914–64)

Choral

A Mighty Fortress Is Our God. For four-part chorus of mixed voices a

cappella. Harmonized and set in anthem form.
R. D. Row Music Co., ©1946.
Carl Fischer, Inc.

Boston Public Library

Negro Spirituals. For four-part chorus of men's voices. Vol. 1 with piano accompaniment, Vol. 2 a cappella. 1. Little David, Play on Your Harp. 2. Them Dry Bones.
R. D. Row Music Co., ©1947.
Carl Fischer, Inc.

Boston Public Library

Piano

Five Sketches.
Handy Bros. Music Co., Inc., ©1947.

Free Library of Philadelphia

SEE: Carl Fischer, Inc.
56–62 Cooper Square
New York, NY 10003

G. Schirmer, Inc.
866 Third Avenue
New York, NY 10022

Handy Bros. Music Co., Inc.
200 West 72nd Street
New York, NY 10023

J. Fischer & Bro.
Belwin-Mills Pub. Corp.
25 Deshon Drive
Melville, NY 11746

S

SAINT-GEORGE, JOSEPH BOULOGNE, CHEVALIER DE (1739–99)

Concertos

Violin Concertos and Two Symphonies Concertantes.
Johnson Reprint Corp., ©1981. OCLC: 8072262.

Arizona State University; Ball State University; Central Missouri State University; Dekalb Community College; Eastern Illinois University Eastman School of Music; Louisiana State University; Miami University, Oxford; Nazareth College; Newberry Library, Chicago; Peabody Institute; Pittsburg State University; Queens College; Smith College; University of Arkansas; University of Kansas; University of Kentucky; University of Vermont, Bailey Library; University of Wisconsin–Milwaukee

Violin No. 1, G Major. For violin and orchestra.
Peer-Southern Organization, ©1975.

Cornell University; University of Arizona; University of Cincinnati

Violin No. 1, G Major. Opus 2. For violin and orchestra.
Peer-Southern Organization ©1975.
OCLC: 2230917.

Arizona State University; Buffalo and Erie County Public Library; College of Wooster; Detroit Public Library; Morgan State University; Temple University; University of California, Los Angeles University of New Mexico; University of Pennsylvania, Philadelphia

Orchestra

Sinfonie Concertante. Opus 13, G Major. For two violins and string orchestra.
Paris: Editions Costallat, ©1966. OCLC: 3233616.

Arizona State University; Boston University; College of Wooster; Cornell University; Detroit Public Library; Duke University Library; Florida State University; Georgia State University; Indiana University; Massachusetts Institute of Technology; Oberlin College; San Francisco State University; University of California, Irvine; University of California, Los Angeles; University of Houston; University of Illinois; University of Michigan

String Quartet

C Major. Opus 1, no. 1. Reconstructed and edited by Dominque-René De Lerma.
Peer-Southern Organization ©1978.
OCLC: 5667246.

Arizona State University; Chicago Public Library; College of Wooster; Indianapolis-Marion County Public Library; Lewis and Clarke College; Massachusetts Institute of Technology; Public Library of Cincinnati and Hamilton County; San Diego State University; SUNY College at Purchase; University of Arizona; University of California, Los Angeles; University of California, Santa Barbara; University of Central Arkansas; University of New Mexico; University of Texas, at Austin; University of Wisconsin–Milwaukee

Vocal

Ernestine. (Opera excerpt.) For soprano with piano accompaniment.
Peer-Southern Organization ©1978.
OCLC: 5982283.

Arizona State University; College of Wooster; Enoch Pratt Free Library, Baltimore; Indiana University; Loyola University of Chicago; Oberlin College; San Diego State University; University of Arizona; University of Cincinnati; University of New Mexico

SCHUYLER, PHILIPPA DUKE (1932–67)

Orchestra

Manhattan Nocturne.
Manuscript.

Yale University, James Weldon Johnson Memorial Collection

The Nile Fantasy. For piano and orchestra. 1. Inshallah or Fate . . . Contemplation and Submission. 2. Violence and Terror. 3. The Long Road to Peace. Arranged by Margaret A. Bonds.

Scherzo.

Sleepy Hollow Sketches.

Piano

Eight Little Pieces.

Nine Little Pieces. Fourth edition. ©1938.

Yale University, James Weldon Johnson Memorial Collection

Rumpelstiltskin.
Buenos Aires: Ricordi Americana, ©1955.

Yale University, James Weldon Johnson Memorial Collection

Three Little Pieces, ©1938.

Yale University, James Weldon Johnson Memorial Collection

The White Nile Suite. Musical saga depicting Arab history in Egypt and the Sudan.

Vocal

African Rhapsody.

Around the World Suite.

Chisamharu the Nogomo.

Country Boy. Juan Hines arrangement.

Cynthia. Juan Hines arrangement.

The Legend of Mahdi. Based on themes from Omdurman, Sudan.

The Rhapsody of Youth.

SIMPSON, EUGENE THAMON (1932–)

Choral

Sinnuh, Please Don't Let Dis Harves' Pass.
For four-part chorus of mixed voices a cappella.
Bourne Co. Music Pub., ©1976. OCLC: 9737142.

Southern Baptist Theological Seminary

SEE: Murbo Music Pub. Inc.
Bourne Company
Music Publishers
1212 Avenue of the Americas
New York, NY 10036

SIMPSON, RALPH RICARDO (1935–)

SEE: Ralph. R. Simpson
Music Department
Tennessee State University
3500 John A. Merritt Blvd.
Nashville, TN 37203

SINGLETON, ALVIN (?)

Cello

Argoru II. Solo cello.
Reproduction of manuscript, ©1971.

New York Public Library

SMITH, HALE, JR. (1925–)

SEE: Belwin-Mills Pub. Corp.
1776 Broadway
New York, NY 10019

C. F. Peters Corp.
373 Park Avenue South
New York, NY 10016

Edward B. Marks Music Corp.
1790 Broadway
New York, NY 10019

Galaxy Music Corp.
131 West 86th Street, Ninth floor
New York, NY 10024

Independent Press
Brodt Music Company
P.O. Box 1207
Charlotte, NC 28231

Theodore Presser Co.
Presser Place
Bryn Mawr, PA 19010

SMITH, NATHANIEL CLARK (1877–1935)

Book

The Elements of Music. A short method of instruction in the rudiments of music and the art of singing by note. Compiled and arranged by N. C. Smith.

Tuskegee Institute, Hollis Burke Frissell Library

Orchestra

Negro Folk Suite.

Piano

Negro Folk Suite. 1. Banana Walk (St. Hele Island). 2. Orange Dance (British Guinea). 3. Pineapple Lament (Martinique). Lyon & Healy.

Newberry Library, Chicago

Vocal

Plantation Song Cycle. For baritone.

For Not Known

Fantasia on "Steal Away to Jesus," a Negro spiritual.

Negro Folk Song Prelude.

Some Favorite Melodies.

Swing Low, Sweet Chariot. Negro spiritual.

SMITH, WARREN I., JR. (1934–)

SEE: Music For Percussion, Inc.
17 West 60th Street
New York, NY 10023

SMITH, WILLIAM HENRY (1908–44)

Choral

Didn't My Lord Deliver Daniel? For four-part chorus of mixed voices a cappella.
Neil A. Kjos Music Co., ©1938.

Hebrew Union College

Smith Book of Spirituals. For four-part chorus of mixed voices. Arranged by W. H. Smith. Edited by Max Thomas Krone.
Neil A. Kjos Music Co., ©1937. OCLC: 9677705.

Boston University, University of Miami Music Library, Coral Gables

SOUTHALL, MITCHELL BERNARD (1922–)

Piano

Elf Dance.
G. Schirmer, Inc., ©1947.

Improptu Militaire.
G. Schirmer, Inc., ©1950.

SEE: Carl Fischer, Inc.
56–62 Cooper Square
New York, NY 10003

G. Schirmer, Inc.
866 Third Avenue
New York, NY 10022

Handy Bros. Music Co., Inc.
200 West 72nd Street
New York, NY 10023

Ralph Jusko Publications, Inc.
Willis Music Co.
7380 Industrial Road
Florence, KY 41042

SOWANDE, FELA (1905–)

Orchestra

African Suite. For strings with full score.
Chappell & Co., Inc. OCLC: 5180076.

University of Texas at Austin

Nigerian Folk Symphony.
Leeds Music Corp.
Belwin-Mills Pub. Corp.

Nigerian Minatures.
London: Performing Right Society Ltd.

Organ

Chorale Preludes on Sacred Yoruba Melodies.
London: Novello & Co., Ltd.

Gloria.
G. Ricordi & Co.
Belwin-Mills Pub. Corp.

Go Down, Moses.
Chappell & Co., Inc.

Jesu Olugbala.
Novello & Co., Ltd.

Joshua Fit de Battle ob Jericho.
Chappell & Co., Inc.

Jubilate.
Manuscript.

K'A Mo Rokoso.
Manuscript.

K'A Mura.
Novello & Co., Ltd.

Kyrie.
Chappell & Co., Inc., ©1955

Obangiji.
Chappell & Co., Inc.

Oyigiyigi.
G. Ricordi & Co.
Belwin-Mills Pub. Corp.

Prayer.
G. Ricordi & Co.
Belwin-Mills Pub. Corp.

SEE: Belwin-Mills Pub. Corp.
1776 Broadway
New York, NY 10019

Chappell & Co., Inc.
810 Seventh Avenue
New York, NY 10019

Novello Publications, Inc.
145 Palisade Street
Dobbs Ferry, NY 10522

The Performing Right Society Ltd.
29/33 Berners Street
London W1P 4AA

STILL, WILLIAM GRANT (1895–1978)

Orchestra

Darker America.
Eastman School of Music, ©1928. OCLC: 4700252.

Boston Public Library; New York Public Library; Newberry Library, Chicago; University of Michigan; University of Texas at Austin

Dismal Swamp. New Music Edition, 1937.
Theodore Presser Co.

Edwin A. Fleisher Music Collection; Yale University, James Weldon Johnson Memorial Collection

Ebon Chronicle

Edwin A. Fleisher Music Collection

From the Journal of a Wanderer.

Edwin A. Fleisher Music Collection

From the Land of Dreams. For chamber orchestra.

In Memoriam: The Colored Soldiers Who Died for Democracy.
Delkas Music Pub. Co., ©1943.
Belwin-Mills Pub. Corp.

Yale University, James Weldon Johnson Memorial Collection

Kaintuck. (Colloquial expression for Kentucky.) Piano and orchestra.

Edwin A. Fleisher Music Collection; Yale University, James Weldon Johnson Memorial Collection

Lenox Avenue.
J. Fischer & Bro.
Belwin-Mills Pub. Corp.

Pages from Negro History. In: *Music of our times; Twelve Orchestra Compositions by American Contempories.* Listed under Robert Guym McBride. Editor: Karl Van Duawe Hoessen. Carl Fischer, Inc., ©1943. Publ. pl. no. 29407–80. OCLC: 1053816.

Catholic University; Edinboro State College; SUNY College of Fredonia; University of Tampa

Scherzo. From *The Afro-American Symphony.* Reduced for small orchestra. J. Fischer & Bro.
Belwin-Mills Pub. Corp.

Three Dances.

Edwin A. Fleisher Music Collection

Organ

Elegy.
Western International Music, Inc.

Reveries.
F. Rayner Brown.

Summerland. Arranged by Edouard Niles-Berger.
J. Fischer & Bro., ©1944.
Baldwin-Mills Pub. Corp.

Cleveland Public Library

Piano

Quit Dat Foolishness.
J. Fischer & Bro.
Belwin-Mills Pub. Corp.

SEE: Bourne Company
Music Publishers
1212 Avenue of the Americas
New York, NY 10036

F. Rayner Brown
2423 Panorama Terrace
Los Angeles, CA 90039

Gemini Music Co.
2122 Massachusetts Ave. N.W.
Washington, D.C. 20008

Handy Brothers Music Co., Inc.
200 West 72nd Street
New York, NY 10023

J. Fischer & Bro.
Belwin-Mills Pub. Corp.
1776 Broadway
New York, New York 10019

M. Witmark & Sons.
Warner Bros. Pub., Inc.
75 Rockefeller Plaza
New York, NY 10019

Peer-Southern Organization
1740 Broadway
New York, NY 10019

Theodore Presser Co.
Presser Place
Bryn Mawr, PA 19010

William Grant Still Music
26892 Preciados Drive
Mission Viejo, CA 92691

SWANSON, HOWARD (1907–78)

Cello

Suite.
Weintraub Music Co., ©1951.

Kansas State Teachers College of Emporia; Miami University, Oxford; New York Public Library; Northwestern University; University of Chicago; University of Cincinnati; University of Southern California

Choral

Nightingales. For four-part chorus of men's voices a cappella. Text by Robert Bridges.
Weintraub Music Co., ©1952.

Boston Public Library

Concerto

Orchestra.
Weintraub Music Co., ©1970.

Orchestra

Music for Strings.
Weintraub Music Co., ©1952.

Symphony No. 1.
Weintraub Music Co., ©1945.

Symphony No. 2. (Short.) Minature score.
Weintraub Music Co., ©1951.

Boston Public Library; Florida State University; New York Public Library; Newberry Library, Chicago; Occidental College; U.S. Library of Congress; University of Cincinnati; University of New Mexico; University of Okalhoma; Yale University, James Weldon Johnson Memorial Collection

Piano

The Cuckoo. Scherzo.
Leeds Music Corp., ©1949.
Belwin-Mills Pub. Corp.

Florida State University; New York Public Library; Northwestern University

Sonata.
Weintraub Music Co., ©1950.

Florida State University; New York Public Library; Peabody Institute; University of Cincinnati; University of Illinois; University of New Mexico; University of Washington, Seattle; Yale University, James Weldon Johnson Memorial Collection

Quintet

Soundpiece. For brass: horn, trombone, trumpets (2), tuba.
Weintraub Music Co., ©1953.

String Octet

Vista No. II.
Weintraub Music Co., ©1969.

Trio

For flute, oboe, and piano.
Weintraub Music Co., ©1975.

Violin

Nocturne. Piano accomaniment.
Weintraub Music Co., ©1951.

Vocal

Cahoots. For medium voice with piano accompaniment. Text by Carl Sandburg.
Weintraub Music Co., ©1951.

A Death Song. Lullaby. For low voice with piano accompaniment. Text by Paul Lawrence Dunbar.
Leeds Music Corp., ©1951.
Belwin-Mills Pub. Corp.

Fantasy Piece. For soprano, saxophone, and strings.
Weintraub Music Co., ©1969.

Four Preludes. For high voice with piano accompaniment. Text by Thomas Elliot Stearns.
Weintraub Music Co., ©1952.

Ghost in Love. For medium voice with piano accompaniment. Text by Vachel Linsay.
Weintraub Music Co., ©1950.

Northwestern University; University of Illinois; University of Texas, Austin; Yale University, James Weldon Johnson Memorial Collection

I Will Lie Down in Autumn. For voice with piano accompaniment. Text by Mary Swenson.
Weintraub Music Co., ©1952.

Yale University, James Weldon Johnson Memorial Collection

In Time of Silver Rain. For high voice with piano accompaniment. Text by Langston Hughes.
Weintraub Music Co., ©1950.

University of Illinois; Yale University, James Weldon Johnson Memorial Collection

Joy. For low voice with piano accompaniment. Text by Langston Hughes.
Leeds Music Corp., ©1950.
Belwin-Mills Pub. Corp.

New York Public Library; University of Illinois; University of Oregon; Yale University, James Weldon Johnson Memorial Collection

The Junk Man. For voice with piano accompaniment. Text by Carl Sandburg.
Weintraub Music Co., ©1950.

New York Public Library; Yale University, James Weldon Johnson Memorial Collection

The Negro Speaks of Rivers. For low voice with piano accompaniment. Text by Langston Hughes.
Leeds Music Corp., ©1949.
Belwin-Mills Pub. Corp.

New York Public Library; University of Illinois; University of Oregon; University of Texas, Austin; Yale University, James Weldon Johnson Memorial Collection

Night Song. For voice with piano accompaniment. Text by Langston Hughes.
Weintraub Music Co., ©1950.

Boston Public Library; New York Public Library; Northwestern University; University of Texas, Austin

113

Pierrot. For voice with piano accompaniment. Text by Langston Hughes
Weintraub Music Co., ©1950.

Yale University, James Weldon Johnson Memorial Collection

Saw a Grave upon a Hill. For voice with piano accompaniment. Text by
Mary Swenson.
Weintraub Music Co., ©1952.

Yale University, James Weldon Johnson Memorial Collection

Snowdunes. For voice with piano accompaniment. Text by Mary Swenson.
Weintraub Music Co., ©1955.

New York Public Library

Songs for Patricia. For high voice with accompaniment. Text by Norman
Rosten.
Weintraub Music Co., ©1952.

New York Public Library; U.S. Library of Congress; University of Cincinnati; University of Florida; Yale University, James Weldon Johnson Memorial Collection

Still Life. For medium voice with piano accompaniment. Text by Carl
Sandburg.
Weintraub Music Co., ©1950.

Northwestern University

To Be or Not to Be. For voice with piano accompaniment. Text anonymous.
Weintraub Music Co., ©1951.

Yale University, James Weldon Johnson Memorial Collection

The Valley. For medium voice with piano accompaniment. Text by Edwin Markham.
Leeds Music Corp., ©1951.
Belwin-Mills Pub. Corp.

New York Public Library; University of Oregon; University of Texas, Austin

Woodwinds

Night Music. For woodinds. horn, and strings. Miniature score.
Weintraub Music Co., ©1951.

Florida State University; New York Public Library; Newberry Library, Chicago;

T

TALBERT, WENDELL P. (?–1950)

Choral

Deep River. Negro spiritual. For chorus of mixed voices.
Handy Bros. Music Co., Inc., ©1934.

TAYLOR, JEAN (?)

Vocal

Kerless Love. Negro song. For voice.
H. W. Gray Co. Inc., ©1928.
Belwin-Mills Pub. Corp.

University of Illinois

Six Negro Spirituals. Collected and arranged for voice with piano accompaniment. 1. Bear Yo' Burden. 2. How Long, Laz' rus? 3. Open de Window, Noah! 4. Plenty o' Room. 5. Sister Mary Wo' Three Lengths of Chain. 6. Soon One Mawnin'.
H. W. Gray Co. Inc., ©1925.
Belwin-Mills Pub. Corp.

New York Public Library; University of New Mexico; Yale University, James Weldon Johnson Memorial Collection

TAYLOR, MAUDE CUMMINGS (1897–)

Choral

How Beautiful upon the Mountains. For four-part chorus of mixed voices with soprano and tenor solos. Piano or organ accompaniment.
Handy Bros. Music Co., Inc., ©1964.

I Will Lift Up Mine Eyes. For four-part chorus of mixed voices with piano accompaniment.
Boston Music Co., ©1961.

They Shall Run and Not Be Weary. For four-part chorus of mixed voices with tenor solo. Piano or organ accompaniment. Henri Elkan Music Pub., ©1960.

TERRY, J. ROY (?)

Organ

Sonata in D Minor.
Manuscript.

THOMAS, ALFRED JACK (1884–1962)

For Not Known

Etude en Noire.

The Sons of Liberty March.

THOMAS, BLANCHE KATURAH (1885–1977)

Piano

Plantation Songs. In easy arrangement.
G. Schirmer, Inc., ©1937.

Tacoma Public Library

THOMAS, C. EDWARD (1935–)

Choral

Let Us Break Bread Together. Negro spiritual. For four-part chorus of mixed voices a cappella.
Beacon Hill Music, ©1974. OCLC: 1598164.

Southern Baptist Theological Seminary

Rock Him. Christmas music. For four-part chorus of mixed voices with piano accompaniment.
Reproduced from holograph. OCLC: 8182477.

Bethel College Learning Resources Center

Sometimes I Feel like a Motherless Child. Negro spiritual. For four-part chorus of mixed voices a cappella.
Beacon Hill Music, ©1974. OCLC: 1464664.

Southern Baptist Theological Seminary

THOMAS, CARLETTE CATHERINE (?)

Choral

Fool That I Am. For four-part chorus of men's voices with piano accompaniment. Words by William Cartwright.
G. Ricordi & Co. Inc., ©1934. Publ. pl. no. N.Y. 963.
Belwin-Mills Pub. Co.

New York Public Library

TILLIS, FREDERICK CHARLES (1930–)

Organ

Passacaglia in Baroque Style.
Manuscript, ©1972.

Three Chorale Settings in Baroque Style.
Manuscript, ©1962.

Woodwinds

For bassoon, clarinet, flute, oboe, percussion.
Microfilm of typescript, Ann Arbor, Michigan, ©1963. OCLC: 1415275.

New Mexico State University

SEE: American Composers Alliance
170 West 74th Street
New York, NY 10023

Peer-Southern Organization
1740 Broadway
New York, NY 10019

TINDLEY, CHARLES ALBERT (1851–1933)

Choral

Leave It There. For four-part chorus of mixed voices, optional solo, with piano accompaniment.
Hope Pub. Co., ©1979. Publ. pl. no. GS826. OCLC: 5767805.

Southern Baptist Theological Seminary

TURKSON, ADOLPHIS (1937–)

Flute

Three Pieces. Opus 14. Piano accompaniment.
Ile-Ife, Nigeria: University of Ife Press, ©1975.

New York Public Library, Schomburg Collection

TYLER, JESSIE GERALD (?)

Vocal

Gerald Tyler's September Musical. Songs and piano numbers.

Oberlin College

For Not Known

Magnificat in E Minor.

Ships That Pass in the Night.

V

VALENTINE, ALEXANDER MARK (1895–)

Band

Southern Memories.
Handy Bros. Music Co., Inc.

Southland Memories.
George F. Brigel.

W

WALKER, GEORGE THEOPHILUS (1922–)

Organ

Choral prelude: Liebster Jesu, Wir Sind Hier (Blessed Jesus, We Are Here).
Manuscript.

Elevation.
Manuscript.

Invocation.
Manuscript.

Violin

Sonata No. 2. Piano accompaniment.
Associated Music Pub. Inc., ©1966.

OCLC

SEE: Associated Music Pub., Inc.
G. Schirmer, Inc.
866 Third Avenue
New York, NY 10022

Galaxy Music Corp.
131 West 86th Street
Ninth floor
New York, NY 10024

New Valley Music Press
Sage Hall 21
Smith College
Northampton, MA 01060

WALTERS, REGINALD G. (1948–)

Piano

Libertas. Opus no. 16.

SEE: Reginald G. Walters
6606 Shirley Avenue
Prospect, KY 40059

WHALUM, WENDELL PHILLIPS (1931–)
SEE: Lawson Gould Music Pub., Inc.
G. Schirmer, Inc.
866 Third Avenue
New York, NY 10022

WHITE, CLARENCE CAMERON (1880–1960)

Ballet

A Night in Sans Souci.

Band

Bandanna Sketches. Opus 12. Negro spirituals. Four movements.
Carl Fischer, Inc.

Triumphal March.
Theodore Presser Co.

Book

A New System of One-octave Scale Studies. Both major and minor scales
for the violin.
C. W. Thompson & Co., ©1915.
Boston Music Company.

Boston Public Library; Oberlin College

Cantata

Heritage. For four-part chorus of mixed voices, tenor or soprano solo,
speaking choral group, and orchestra accompaniment. Words by Countee Cullen.
Manuscript, ©1960 (reproduced).

Yale University, James Weldon Johnson Memorial Collection

Choral

Traditional Negro Spirituals. Twenty concert and community pieces. For four-part chorus of mixed voices a cappella.
Carl Fischer, Inc., ©1940. Publ. pl. no. 28854–20. OCLC: 6766682.

Boston Public Library; New York Public Library; Public Library of Cincinnati and Hamilton County; U.S. Library of Congress; Yale University, James Weldon Johnson Memorial Collection

Clarinet

Petite Suite. 1. Capriccietto. 2. Shepherd's Serenade. 3. Slumber Song. Piano accompaniment.
Sam Fox Pub. Co., Inc., ©1958. OCLC: 7262082.

SUNY College at Fredonia

Suite Spirituale. For four B-flat clarinets.
Henri Elkan Music Pub., ©1956. OCLC: 7663931.

East Carolina University

Concerto

E Minor. No. 2.

G Minor. Opus 63.

U.S. Library of Congress

Opera

Ouanga. A Haitian opera in three acts. Libretto by John Frederick Matheus. English words. Piano-vocal score.
Sam Fox Pub. Co., Inc., ©1955.

Boston Public Library; New York Public Library; U.S. Library of Congress

——————————. Facsimile of piano-vocal score.

Florida State University, Tallahassee

Orchestra

Bandanna Sketches. Opus 12. Negro spirituals. Four movements.
Carl Fischer, Inc.

Dance Rhapsody.

Divertimento.
Sam Fox Pub. Co., Inc.

Elegy. RO-W77.
Carl Fischer, Inc.

From the Cotton Fields. Opus 18. Negro spirituals. Three movements.
Carl Fischer, Inc.

From the Cotton Fields. Opus 18, no. 2 On the Bayou. Negro spiritual.
Arranged by Charles J. Roberts.
Carl Fischer, Inc.

Boston Public Library; University of Oklahoma

Kutumba (Kwtamba). Opus 50.
Sam Fox Pub. Co., Inc.

Pantomime. Opus 36.

Piece for Strings and Timpani.
Sam Fox Pub. Co., Inc.

Poeme.

Prelude to Ouanga. Full score.
Manuscript.

Yale University, James Weldon Johnson Memorial Collection

Suite on Negro Folk Tunes. Four movements.
Sam Fox Pub. Co., Inc.

Tambour (Haitian Dance). Opus 34.
Sam Fox Pub. Co., Inc.

Organ

Triumphal March. Arranged by A. H. Ryder.
Theodore Presser Co., ©1928.

Curtis Institute of Music

Piano

Clouds.

Dance Caprice. Opus 60, no. 3.
Boston Music Company.

University of Illinois

Improvisation.

Kashmirian Dance.

Reflets. Opus 24, no. 1.
Theodore Presser Co., ©1925

University of Illinois

Triumphal March. Opus 30.
Theodore Presser Co., ©1927.

Boston Public Library

String Quartet

String Quartet.

Violin

Bandanna Sketches. Opus 12, no. 1. Chant. Nobody Knows de Trouble
I've Seen. Piano accompaniment.
Carl Fischer, Inc., ©1918. OCLC: 5429822.

*Carnegie-Mellon University; North Texas State University; Cleveland Public
Library*

Bandanna Sketches. Opus 12. Negro spirituals. Piano accompaniment.
Carl Fischer, Inc., ©1918. OCLC: 2666514.

Duquesne University Library

Cradle Song (Berceuse). Opus 10, no. 1. Piano accompaniment.
Boston Music Company.

Four Pieces. 1. Caprice. 2. Serenade. 3. Twilight. 4. Valse Coquette.
Carl Fischer, Inc., ©1922. Publ. pl. nos. 22434–7.

New York Public Library

From the Cotton Fields. Opus 18. Negro spirituals. Cabin Song. On the
Bayou. Piano accompaniment.
Carl Fischer, Inc., ©1920–26.

Levee Dance. Opus 26, no. 2. Piano accompaniment.
Carl Fischer, Inc., ©1927.

Boston Public Library

Negro Dance. Sometimes I Feel like a Motherless Child. Piano accompaniment.
Carl Fischer, Inc.

Scotch Idyl.
Carl Fischer, Inc.

Springtide. An arrangement of Edvard Grieg's piece.
Theodore Presser Co.

Steal Away. Negro spiritual.
Theodore Presser Co.

Vocal

Cabin Memories. Negro spirituals. For voice with piano accompaniment.
1. Bear the Burden. 2. Down by de Ribber Side. 3. I'm Goin' Home.
Carl Fischer, Inc., ©1926.

New York Public Library

5 Songs. Opus 39. For high voice with piano accompaniment. 1. Bend
Down, Beloved. 2. Deliverance. 3. Nay, Do Not Weep. 4. Overtones.
5. Worship.
Sam Fox Pub. Co., Inc., ©1949.

Hear the Good News. For voice with piano accompaniment.

For Not Known

Five Songs. 1. Camp. 2. Fleurette. 3. Improvisation. 4. Levee Dance.
5. Plantation Song.

WHITE, DON LEE (?)

Organ

By the Waters of Babylon.
Manuscript.

Christmas Fantasy.
Manuscript.

Jesus, Keep Me Near the Cross.
Manuscript.

Magnificat.
Manuscript, ©1961.

Thanksgiving Fantasy.
Manuscript, ©1966.

SEE: Don Lee White
4144 West 62nd Street
Los Angeles, CA 90043

WHITE, JOSEPH (1833–1920)

Concerto

F-sharp Violin and orchestra. Revised and edited by Paul Glass and Kermit Moore. Piano reduction by John Ruggero. Belwin-Mills Pub. Corp., ©1976. OCLC: 2835045.

New York Public Library; University of New Mexico

SEE: OCLC

Violin

La Jota Aragonesa. Opus 5. Caprice. Piano accompaniment. Edited by Paul Glass.
Associated Music Publishers, Inc., ©1975. OCLC: 2068052.

University of New Mexico

SEE: OCLC

WHITING, HELEN ADELE JOHNSON (1885–)

Songs

Negro Art, Music and Rhyme. For young folks. Illustrations by Lois Mailou Jones. Book II.
The Associated Pub., Inc., ©1938. OCLC: 1445239, 1746570.

Boston Public Library; Cleveland Public Library; Duke University; Free Library of Philadelphia; Howard University; New York Public Library; U.S. Library of Congress; University of Colorado; University of Georgia; Spokane Public Library; University of Tennessee

Other locations, see: OCLC

WILLIAMS, ANDREW THOMAS (?)

Piano

Seven Preludes. Opus 1. Rhythme d' Afrique.
E. Schuberth & Co., ©1924. Publ. pl. no. E.S. & Co. 4437.

New York Public Library

Violin

Muezzin. Piano accompaniment.
E. Schuberth & Co., ©1924

WILLIAMS, ARNOLD K. (1928–)

SEE: Plymouth Music Co. Inc.
170 NE 33 Street
Fort Lauderdale, FL 33334

WILLIAMS, JULIUS P., JR. (1954–)

Organ

Sounds of Colors.
Manuscript.

SEE: Julius P. Williams Jr.
43 Fountain Avenue
Middletown, CT 06457

WILSON, OLLY WOODROW (1937–)

Organ

Expansions.
Manuscript, ©1979.

SEE: Olly W. Wilson
Department of Music
University of California
Berkeley, CA 94704

WISNER, GENEVIEVE MCVEY (1907–)

For Not Known

Compensation.

Home on a Cloud.

'Round the Throne of God.

WORK, FREDERICK JEROME (1885–1942)

Choral

Folk Songs of the American Negro.
B.Y.P.U. Board.

Brown University; Cleveland Public Library; Duke University; Fisk University; Howard University; New York Public Library; Northwestern University; Oberlin College; Rutgers University; Tennessee State Library and Archives; University of British Columbia; University of Idaho; University of Tennessee; Yale University

New Jubilee Songs. Collected and harmonized by F. J. Work. Fisk University, ©1902.

Denver Public Library; Grosvenor Reference Division, Erie County Public Library, Buffalo; New York Public Library; Oberlin College; Wesleyan University

String Quartet

F Major.

WORK, JOHN W., III (1901–67)

Cantata

The Singers. Based on a poem by Henry Wadsworth Longfellow. For chorus, baritone, and orchestra.
(First prize in 1946 of Fellowship of American Composers.)
Mills Music, Inc., ©1949.
Belwin-Mills Pub. Corp.

Boston Public Library; U.S. Library of Congress

Choral

American Negro Songs. A comprehensive collection of religious and secular folk songs. For chorus of mixed voices.
Theodore Presser Co., ©1948.
SEE: NUC Pre-1956 Imprints volume 674, page 46.
Yale University, James Weldon Johnson Memorial Collection

Danse Africaine. For four-part chorus of mixed voices with soprano solo, piano, tambourine, triangle, and two drums. Poem by Langston Hughes. Ethel Smith Music Corp., ©1951.

Yale University, James Weldon Johnson Memorial Collection

How Beautiful upon the Mountains. For four-part chorus of mixed voices a cappella.
Galaxy Music Corp., ©1934.

Yale University, James Weldon Johnson Memorial Collection

129

Isaac Watts Contemplates the Cross. A choral cycle. For four-part chorus of mixed voices with soprano, alto, tenor, and baritone solos. Piano accompaniment.
Broadman Press, ©1962.
I've Known Rivers. For eight-part chorus of mixed voices a cappella. Poem by Langston Hughes.
Galaxy Music Corp., ©1955.

Yale University, James Weldon Johnson Memorial Collection

Oh! I've Seen Many Mountains. For chorus of mixed voices with soloists. Piano accompaniment. Words by Arna Bontemps and J. W. Work III.
Ethel Smith Music Corp., ©1954.

Yale University, James Weldon Johnson Memorial Collection

Song of the Mississippi Boatman. Adapted from a Negro folk song. For chorus of men's voices.
J. Fischer & Bro., ©1940.
Belwin-Mills Pub. Corp.

Duke University

Orchestra

Night in the Valley.

Taliafero. Overture.

Yenvalou. Haitian themes. (Commissioned for the Saratoga Springs Spa Festival.)
Galaxy Music Corp.

Organ

Five Negro Spirituals. Arrangements. 1. Give Me Jesus. 2. I'm A-rolling through an Unfriendly World. 3. A Little More Faith in Jesus. 4. Sinner Man, You Need Jesus. 5. When Your Lamp Burns Down.
Lorenz Pub. Co.

Picture Suite. From the Deep South: Spiritual, Plaint, A Summer Evening, Frolic.
Manuscript.

Piano

Appalachia. Three fiddle and game tunes.
Axelrod Publications, ©1945.
Shawnee Press, Inc.

Sassafras.
Mercury Music Corp., ©1946.
Theodore Presser Co.

Scuppernog. Three pieces country folk: 1. At a Certain Church. 2. Ring Game. 3. Visitor from Town.
Axelrod Publications.
Shawnee Press, Inc.

Violin

Nocturne. Piano accompaniment.

Vocal

Soliloquy. For voice with piano accompaniment. Lyrics by Myrtle Vorst Sheppard.
Galaxy Music Corp., ©1946.

Ten Spirituals. Arranged for voice with piano accompaniment.
Ethel Smith Music Corp., ©1952.

WORK, JOHN WESLEY, SR. (1871–1925)

Book

Folk Song of the American Negro.
F. A. McKensie, ©1915.
Press of Fisk University.

WORK, JULIAN C. (1910–)

Band

Driftwood Patterns. Symphonic. Condensed score.
Shawnee Press, Inc., ©1961. OCLC: 2211838.

Northern Kentucky State College

Moses. From *Portraits from the Bible*. Symphonic.
Shawnee Press, Inc.

Processional Hymn. Symphonic.
Shawnee Press, Inc.

Ruth. From *Portaits from the Bible*. Symphonic.
Shawnee Press, Inc.

Stand the Storm. Symphonic.
Shawnee Press, Inc.

Orchestra

Myriorama by Night. Suite in four movements.
Manuscript.

NAME INDEX

135

SUBJECT INDEXES

138

139

140

Still, William Grant (1895–1978), 110
White, Clarence Cameron (1880–1960), 123

OPERETTA

Barbour, J. Berni (1881–), 7
Dennis, Norton Edward (?), 33
Johnson, Hall (1888–1970), 65
Morgan, William Astor (Pseudonym: Jean Stor) (1890–?), 83

ORATORIO

Brown, J. Harold (1902–), 15
De Paur, Leonard (1914–), 32
Dett, Robert Nathaniel (1882–1943), 33
Jessye, Eva Alberta (1895–), 62
King, Betty Jackson (1928–), 71

GOSPEL

Dorsey, Thomas Andrew (1899–), 37
Tindley, Charles Albert (1851–1933), 118

LITURGICAL MASS

McLin, Lena Johnson (1928–), 76

MUSIC DRAMA

Pittman, Evelyn La Rue (1910–), 91

MUSICAL COMEDY

Boatner, Edward Hammond (1898–1981), 10

ORGAN AND INSTRUMENTS

Fletcher, John (?), 47
Hancock, Eugene Wilson (1929–), 55

ORGAN AND PERCUSSION

Da Costa, Noel George (1929–), 29

ORGAN AND STRINGS

Da Costa, Noel George (1929–), 29

PIANO

Anderson, Thomas Jefferson, Jr. (1928–), 3
Baker, David Nathaniel, Jr. (1931–), 5
Bankole, Ayo (1935–1976), 6
Barès, Basile J. (1845–1902), 6–7
Barnes, Erik S. (1955–), 8
Beckon, Lettie Marie (1953–), 8
Bethune, Thomas Green (1849–1908), 8
Bonds, Margaret Allison (1913–1972), 12
Charlton, Melville, (1880–1973), 19
Coleridge-Taylor, Samuel (1875–1912), 24
Cordero, Roque (1917–), 27
Dawson, William Levi (1899–), 32
Dett, Robert Nathaniel (1882–1943), 34
Diton, Carl Rossini (1886–1962), 36
El-Dabh, Halim (1921–),40
Elie, Justin (1883–1931), 42
Euba, Akin (1935–), 43
Fax, Mark (1911–1974), 46
Harris, Ethel Ramos (?), 56
Johnson, John Rasamond (1873–1954), 66
Kay, Ulysses Simpson (1917–), 69
King, Betty Jackson (1928–), 71
Lamothe, Ludovic (1882–1953), 72
Lewis, Frederick Elliot (1846–?), 74
Lloyd, Charles, Jr. (1948–), 74
McCarty, Victor Eugene (1821–circa 1890), 76
McDaniel, William Foster (1940–), 76
McSwain, Augusta Geraldine (1917–), 77
Moffat, Richard Cullen (1927–1982), 80
Norman, Jeannette Latimer (?), 86
Perkinson, Coleridge-Taylor (1932–), 88
Price, Florence Beatrice Smith (1888–1953), 93–95
Reece, Donald Cortez (1910–1974), 97
Roldan, Amadeo (1900–1939), 99
Ryder, Noah Francis (1914–1964), 100
Schuyler, Philippa Duke (1932–1967), 103
Smith, Hale, Jr. (1925–), 104–105
Smith, Nathaniel Clark (1877–1935), 105
Southall, Mitchell Bernard (1922–), 106
Still, William Grant (1895–1978), 109
Swanson, Howard (1907–1978), 111
Thomas, Blanche Katurah (1885–1977), 117
Walker, George Theophilus (1922–), 121
Walters, Reginald G. (1948–), 122
White, Clarence Cameron (1880–1960), 124–125

141

142